MILITARY ARCHAEOLOGY

A collectors' guide to 20th Century war relics

Companion volumes

Aviation Archaeology

A collectors' guide to aeronautical relics: airfields,
autographs, badges, books, nomenclature, postcards,
propellers, records, research, stamps and wrecks.
by Bruce Robertson

Epics of Aviation Archaeology
by Bruce Robertson

MILITARY ARCHAEOLOGY

A collectors' guide to 20th Century war relics

Terry Gander

 Patrick Stephens, Cambridge

First published in 1979

British Library Cataloguing in Publication Data

Gander, Terence John
    Military archaeology
    1. Military paraphernalia—Collectors and collecting
    I. Title
    355.8'09'04   U790

    ISBN 0 85059 302 6

Text photoset in 10 on 11pt English 50
by Stevenage Printing Limited, Stevenage.
Printed in Great Britain (on 100 gsm
Fineblade Cartridge) and bound by
The Garden City Press, Letchworth, for
the publishers, Patrick Stephens Limited,
Bar Hill, Cambridge, CB3 8EL, England.

Contents

Foreword

I must confess to having experienced some difficulty in believing my own hearing when Terry Gander asked me whether I would write a Foreword for this book. As someone who has crept in through the back of military archaeology via model making and wargaming, it struck me that any contribution I could make would be rather presumptuous.

I have known Terry for many years now, and his in-depth knowledge of military affairs has been of great personal help on numerous occasions at military rallies and on Army exercises. In the interim, we have often discussed many of the subjects dealt with in this book, and I am certain his advice will prove of as much value to other readers as to myself.

To give just a couple of examples: first, photographic interpretation. As an author, my own work frequently takes me to the Bundesarchiv in Germany (where one is at least fortunate in that one is working from the original negatives, unretouched by any censor). But there are vast problems in identifying much of the material, and especially in allocating dates and situations. Recently, Terry's critical methods revealed a sequence of photographs of SS 'Das Reich' vehicles which have usually been captioned 'winter 1943-1944' because they bear the so-called 'Kursk' markings, whilst in fact they come in sequence with other photographs taken during the Kharkov operation in early 1943, indicating that the 'Kursk' marking was applied earlier than is normally thought. The clear lesson is—don't believe what other people say, even in the most authoritative-looking books!

Similarly, the chapters on military architecture have opened my eyes to the various structures in the vicinity of my home, and made me look with fresh interest and knowledge at coastal fortifications discovered whilst on holiday. (As an aside, I think the Channel Islands Tourist Board ought to pay Terry a royalty for the flood of new visitors this book should inspire!)

Joking apart, the field of military archaeology embraces so many different and fascinating forms of activity that the newcomer will inevitably find it hard to distinguish the wood from the trees. This book, providing as it does a clear guide to each of the main fields of endeavour, will be of especial value to the novice, although the experienced researcher and collector will find it of immense interest—and there are many self-professed 'experts' who would do well to read it equally thoroughly!

It has been a privilege to act as the editor of this fine book and a pleasure to contribute these few short words to a volume which will unquestionably make a significant addition to the collections of all genuine military enthusiasts and become a standard reference work for many years to come.

Cambridge, 1978   *Bruce Quarrie*

Introduction

Without being aware of the fact I have been involved in some form or another of military archaeology for as long as I can remember. To this day I have a large and unsorted collection of cap badges that was first formed when I was about six years old. My library still has several tatty volumes which were first placed on my book pile when I was around ten. When I was about 14 I was given my first box camera and from then onwards I have been pointing a succession of cameras at military subjects. In total my contacts with the military world have been many but until recently my many and varied interests have had one thing in common—they have all been totally disorganised and unco-ordinated. Items were collected and stored, often in unsuitable conditions or in locations which rendered them invisible until they re-emerged several years or house moves later. Being so disorganised, and possessing a mental condition which can only be compared with that of a squirrel in autumn, my various collections, be they of books, artefacts or data, have grown and grown over the years—much to the dismay of my long-suffering wife and to the great delight of various forms of insect life that assemble whenever my hoard is put to rest. Only lately have I managed to get part of my library in order and even now, when I can at last consider myself to be at least partially organised, there is still much sorting and compiling to carry out—and still my collections grow.

If it can ever be said that there was a point in my life when I started to view my progress till then as rather a shambles, it can be said to have come about while I was on the pleasant island of Jersey about five or six years ago. I had been writing to a Mr Michael Ginns for some time when he invited me to visit the island and see the sites left in the wake of the German Occupation of 1940 to 1945. Until then I had little idea of what I would actually be seeing and had vague notions of damp and dirty wrecks of bunkers choked with debris and rubbish. Some of the sites I saw were like that but some amazed me. The best of these was the site of a battery of 15.5 cm French guns at Les Landes, in the north-west corner of Jersey. The battery had been emplaced in large concrete circular pits with the guns resting on steel platforms pivoted in the centre of each pit to give a full 360 degree traverse. My amazement was due to the fact that after more than 30 years those gun emplacements were still in a condition which could only be described as excellent. The years had taken their toll with such items as rusted metalwork and many of the surrounding shelters and magazines were dilapidated and stripped of anything which might be considered remotely useful, but my imagination was stirred by the sight of those gun positions that looked as though the guns could be put back into action with only a minimum of effort—sadly the guns were in the sea at the foot of nearby cliffs.

Having seen those emplacements, I wanted to know more, and as is usual in so many similar cases, someone had been there before me. There was no one individual involved but rather a whole group of them, even if it did seem that Michael Ginns was the one imparting the information to me personally. The group involved was the

Channel Islands Occupation Society (CIOS from here on) with branches in Jersey and Guernsey. Many of these people went to great lengths to tell me the history of the German Occupation and I tried to soak in as much as possible, especially regarding the weapons which are still my prime interest in the period. What came over time and again was the sensible way the CIOS had managed to organise and carry out its research. It seemed that no detail was too small to omit or no obstacle too large to overcome in the effort to chronicle the Islands' story, and as a result the society had carried out a great deal of excellent work which deserved a better coverage. Since then much of the CIOS work has been presented to a much wider audience and it is now getting some of the recognition it deserves.

After that first visit to Jersey I have been back many times but the impressions made then still remain. Perhaps the most lasting impression has been made on my own working and collecting methods. At long last the CIOS had brought home to me the importance of a properly thought-out and controlled method of putting my house in order (in more ways than one!). At the same time I had been further impressed by the fact that, although World War 2 ended but a few years ago, in only a relatively few locations are there any tangible relics to be seen. Military structures are often intended to be temporary but many of the more robust structures have already succumbed to the elements or 're-development'. It did not take me very long to recognise that this gradual and seemingly ever-increasing erosion of relics of warfare is not confined to structures. All manner of items from vehicles and uniforms to books and diaries are being consigned to scrapheaps and dustbins. Much of this material is irreplaceable and much of it has gone already. Some sort of effort must be made *now* before it is altogether too late to preserve and collect/record what is left.

The above deals only with buildings and artefacts but the most important items have not yet been mentioned: the memories of the people who went through either or both of the two greatest wars the world has ever known. Out of the unknown millions who experienced those conflicts only a statistical handful have ever left any record in print, tape or film. It is true that many had (or felt they had) little to say but today such an attitude is under review. What little is now available is usually the legacy of those who were involved in the wars at high levels. The vast bulk of those who were led carried out their mundane everyday military tasks and only a relative few saw actual combat. The time has now come for those multitudes to have some memorial and, as the commercial world of publishing is unlikely to commit funds to what must be an unprofitable venture, the modern military historian must step in and make an attempt to record the activities of the many in those momentous years. The task will not be an easy one as those who have made the first steps will already have found, but it is a task which must be attempted. Time is not on our side. The veterans of 1914-1918 are now few and far between for the years have taken their toll, and the men and women who went to war in the prime of youth between 1939 and 1945 are now nearly all comfortably middle-aged. Already memories are fading and becoming compressed. If we do not make some record of their achievements future generations will not thank us.

Therefore this book is very much a personal view of what can be done by anyone who has even the most limited resources, but has the interest and will to do his or her own bit in preserving, recording, renovating or collecting something from the debris of two World Wars. I stress that it is very much a personal work as I am well aware that there are many private persons and organised bodies who are already deeply involved in much that I will mention in the following pages. Where possible their name will be mentioned but I know that, very often, their organisational and working methods differ from mine in many ways. What I hope will not differ is the overall objective which is to retain as much of our recent martial past as possible, for future generations to learn from.

What I hope to outline is how all this work should be carried out. I will not attempt to cover every facet of military archaeology—that would involve a volume many sizes larger than this one. Nor can mention be made of every line of research, renovation or collecting related to military archaeology. I must repeat that this book is a personal view of the military archaeology scene and the result of my own contacts, interests and views. Much of it is the end product of amassing a great deal of background information, both published and personal, and the assistance of a large number of people to whom my thanks are due. Much of it is also the end result of a great deal of wasted time and effort caused by my own personal bad organisation which, in its turn, has been productive by my learning how not to go about things. Practical experience gained in writing and researching a number of books on military topics has been invaluable.

Acknowledgements

A book of this nature cannot be written without the assistance and guidance of a number of people. To all of them I offer my thanks, but I am especially grateful to the following:

All the members of the Channel Islands Occupation Society who have given so freely of their time and knowledge. I cannot list them all but mention must be made of Michael Ginns, Colin Partridge and Richard Heaume.

Joe Lyndehurst for allowing me access to his excellent collection and putting up with me at odd times.

Ken Musgrave, not only for running out drawings for me but giving me permission to use some of his photographs.

Henry Wills for his valuable contribution to the pillbox section.

Paul Leaney for his considerable assistance and attentions.

Peter Chamberlain for use of some of his pictures and, as always, for his advice and guidance.

Eric Bull for his considerable contribution to my knowledge of coastal defences.

Paul Wieland for showing me how to use a metal detector to find mortar fuzes.

And all the others who have helped.

Billingshurst, 1978   *Terry Gander*

Chapter 1

A few basic research principles

This chapter has been included as a guide around some of the more basic pitfalls which await anyone who carries out research or investigation into any aspect of military archaeology. It has been based on my own experiences and those of numerous people I have worked with in the past. It has also been based on what I have been able to observe of other persons' and groups' activities, for very often I have seen well-meaning and well-intentioned research projects get bogged down in duplicated and wasted effort, bad feelings, damaged artefacts and, all too often, there has been no worthwhile end product.

One of the most important principles I have learned to adopt before venturing on any new project is, quite simply, wait and think. Before any avenue of military archaeology is entered it would be well worth while to spend a little time considering exactly what you are letting yourself into. All too often this simple step is not taken and in the end you may find yourself in situations which are not congenial to your personality. An example could be that of a young man who commits himself to the excavation or renovation of part of a fortification. Such work is time-consuming and far from clean, although once started it can be absorbing and rewarding. But if that same young man is about to enter the married estate it can also lead to many troubles and recriminations. A simple example perhaps, but one I have seen happen with unpleasant results. Another thing which can happen is that an individual takes on a task that is beyond his personal resources. It may sound like a good idea to discover and list all the serial numbers of the vehicles that landed in Normandy on D-Day, for instance, but to complete a useful and comprehensive tabulation would involve a tremendous amount of time, effort and money. Even in the preliminary stages travel and documentation alone will absorb an alarming amount of cash and once the magnitude of such a project becomes apparent it is only too easy to become discouraged and give up. One is then left with a mass of partly digested material which is of little use to anyone else.

From the two examples quoted above it can be seen that the old military maxim 'time spent in reconnaissance is rarely wasted' very much applies to our field. Don't rush into something you may not be able to afford or finish. There are several questions that have to be asked. Can the time be afforded? Can you cover the costs involved? Is there adequate storage space? Will you be able to fully and usefully complete the chosen project? One very important question to be asked is: has anyone else carried out any work on the subject already? This latter point may be obvious but is one that time and time again I have seen forgotten or ignored. It is a galling experience to commence a project only to discover someone has completed it already and almost as bad is to discover that someone is duplicating your efforts. In such a wide field as military archaeology such duplication is frequently unavoidable, but very often a little investigation will prevent a great deal of wasted effort.

The time spent before you commence anything is a very necessary part of any project for it is time spent on planning. In this book planning is a word that pops up frequently for the simple reason that it is essential to any research, investigation, collecting, renovation or preservation task. Without planning such projects very often founder so a short look at some planning basics will not go amiss.

One of the first of these basics is to be quite clear in your mind exactly what it is you wish to achieve—this is your objective. A vague idea along the lines of 'investigating the military relics in my locality' will not be precise enough. Such a vague proposition will soon founder as a little investigation will reveal that your locality contains a whole host of relics of a very varied nature ranging from Iron Age hill forts to World War 2 anti-aircraft sites. In between may be Napoleonic barracks, Tudor gun batteries, World War 1 prisoner-of-war camp sites, and so on. This wide range (and such a range is not uncommon in many parts of the United Kingdom—we have our long and troubled history to thank for that) cannot be usefully covered unless you want to spend the best part of your lifetime in historical research of all kinds, and another point is that you haven't even defined exactly what your locality boundaries are. So, at least in your early stages, be more precise and set yourself an objective which has the following components:

1 Be realistic. Set yourself a task that can be achieved. It would be nice to build up a museum of all the British Army uniforms worn between 1939 and 1945 but not even the Imperial War Museum with all its backing facilities can manage that.
2 Set yourself a reasonable time period, eg, 1939 to 1945, rather than the whole of the 20th Century.
3 Be quite clear what your end product will be, ie, a book, series of articles or a single article, a displayed collection, a structure open to the public or just preserved, and so on.
4 Try to set yourself a time scale to prevent your project seemingly dragging on for ever. This has the added advantage of being used as a yardstick of success or failure. If a time scale of, say, one year is used, at the end of that year one can see exactly how much has been achieved or (more sadly) how little. Re-appraisals of the project can then be made and alternatives taken, if necessary.

The above is only a rough guide to sorting out your objective but it covers the main points. Once an objective is clear the next stage is to sort out your resources—what you have and what you will need. Again, this sounds simple but if this stage is missed it can lead to problems.

High on the list of resources is time—how much have you got and how much will you need? Any branch of military archaeology is very demanding of time and it is well to realise the fact early on and plan accordingly. Very few of us can lavish unlimited time on our hobbies or interests so what little time we have has to be used to the full. Once again we are back to objectives for very often time alone will dictate them. Vehicle preservation is one field where lack of time is frequently a limiting factor—I know of some projects which foundered because preservation time was so limited that precious relics were deteriorating faster than the preservation work could be carried out. An extreme example, perhaps, but it illustrates a point. In many cases how much time will be needed is difficult to foresee—a simple project may turn into a major one whereas a seemingly time-consuming task may be shortened by a chance discovery. Perhaps the best policy is always to overestimate the time you will need.

Another factor which all too often imposes its own parameters is cost. Everyone will have their own individual cost restrictions and they alone will influence the objective. Always try to work out a rough idea of the costs involved before you start. If you are a collector you should have a rough idea of market values before you commence but remember that market values are subject to fluctuations and very rarely these days are such fluctuations downwards. Vehicle and building preservationists can commit themselves to quite considerable outlay only to find themselves in trouble when expensive snags arise so very often it is a good idea to have an emergency fund to fall back on. Researchers will similarly find that travel costs alone will limit their activities—try regular visits to the Public Record Office when you live in the north of Scotland and you will soon see what I mean. Other things such as books, stationery, tools if necessary, and a long list of other expensive items have to be planned for—it is as well to budget for them early if you want your project to have an end result.

Other resources than the above also need to be considered. Space is one essential for most military archaeologists, whatever their interest. Vehicle preservation is one obvious case in point for very often preservation work cannot be carried out in the open and a garage is necessary. I know of several cases where valuable vehicles have stood rotting in the open for lack of suitable cover. Even pure research needs a great deal of space for any researcher will tell you that in a remarkably short space of time any project amasses a whole heap of paperwork, and books and files need shelving. If the space is not available problems soon present themselves and I know of several cases where parental or marital obduracy has led to piles of invaluable material being dumped.

You can soon work out your own list of resources to be considered as each field of military archaeology will impose its own parameters. The main thing is to have them planned in advance.

Once an objective has been set the most important thing is to keep to it. This is not as easy as it sounds, as many who have delved into any sort of project will know. Perhaps an example will illustrate the point. Not very long ago I was carrying out some reading as the background to a listing of the types of coastal defence artillery used by the Japanese between 1941 and 1945. One report I read contained a section on the 'last ditch' defences of the Japanese mainland. One measure to be taken was the use of human *Kamikaze* mines against the expected invasion fleet. These human mines were to be issued with rudimentary diving gear and the idea was they would walk across the sea bottom from the shore carrying explosive charges. Once under a target vessel they would detonate the charge. The report carried a great deal of detail on this extreme defence measure and needless to say I was fascinated and absorbed to the point where the coastal artillery was virtually forgotten and ideas for articles on the human mines almost took over. But I had to return to my original task after all, leaving a mental note of the new-found information for a future date.

To separate this day-to-day task of keeping to the job in hand one has to use the original objective as a control measure. When delving into any task it is good to adopt the principle, from time to time, of examining the work in hand and comparing it with the objective to see if the work or standard is relevant. Not everyone will want to do this but it can act as a useful corrective aid to prevent wasted time or effort. Again, an example may be useful. It may be very interesting to delve into the reasons why a certain heraldic device is contained in a certain regimental badge but prolonged research into the ancient mythological history which produced it is of little avail if you are simply trying to sort out where the regiment was based in 1941. Personally, I don't always find such diversions from my intentions to be fruitless but often such wanderings have been rewarded with little material to show for my pains at the end of the day. Many a researcher will echo my comments, even if it has uncovered fresh fields and pastures new.

Organisation is not a word which many people like to apply to their general hobbies and interests but if military archaeology is to be usefully carried out by even small groups of people, organisation is necessary. Yet again, this may seem to be an obvious statement to make but all too often one finds that not even the most basic organisational principles are applied to group activities and the results are seldom good. When an individual is working alone, self-organisation, such as having the right material and tools ready to hand, is relatively easy, but to ensure the same happens when a major group task has to be carried out calls for rather more effort. I was once involved in the clearing of a site when about 15 people turned up, but not one of them had brought along any clearing tools or shovels—result, no clearing done. The example may once more be thought of as over-simplified but it does illustrate the point that once individuals congregate to work as a group, someone has to organise and issue some form of guidance and directives. The British race usually has a head start in these matters for we are a nation of self-organisers and it usually doesn't take long for any group of interested persons with a common aim to form themselves into some sort of body with their own hierachy and rules. Anyone who has been involved in any such grouping will know that personal problems and difficulties frequently arise, but an effective counter to this argument is that any group without any organisation very soon produces even more troubles. It is no use my trying to outline how this group organisation should be carried out—that is up to each group to sort out for itself. But some form of internal organisation is essential, especially in what I term 'enclosed societies' for it is then that the risk of duplication of effort becomes high. All too often people set off along one avenue of activity blissfully unaware that someone in their own vicinity or group is carrying out the same work. In such circumstances some form of co-ordination post is a must, but just as essential is some form of internal body which has the responsibility not only for working out a set of rules, but also for establishing exactly what the aim or aims of the particular group or organisation is going to be. Just as important as establishing this aim is propagating the fact so that members or new members can be under no illusions as to what they are involved in. Once again we are back to objectives but in a group organisation the importance of clear objectives is even more important than in the individual case. An individual can adapt and alter his course of action without upsetting anyone but himself. A group which is not clear as to why it has been brought together, other than by a vague mutual interest shared among friends or acquaintances, is very likely just to drift along and disintegrate with little achieved other than mutual recriminations and bad feelings.

So there are my three big basics for military archaeology—planning, control and organisation. All three are essential for any course your interests might take, but for me the most important is planning. Many people already employ all three without being really aware of the fact and very often they are the people who produce the best research results, the best turned-out vehicles, the best displays and the best collections. Their opposites, the disorganised, can be spotted very easily—unfortunately their numbers are legion.

Chapter 2

Using museums and libraries

The four nations that make up the present-day United Kingdom all have long and eventful histories which go back many hundreds of years. Despite the ravages of time and events a surprising amount of information and carefully kept artefacts have survived as reminders of our turbulent past. Many of these relics are now stored and displayed in museums and, indeed, some of them *are* museums. Examples of this latter can be found at the Rotunda Museum at Woolwich and Fort Widley in the Hillsea Lines above Portsmouth Harbour. In our own area of interest, two World Wars and many other more modest campaigns have produced vast quantities of historical material which have found their way into museums and libraries all over the country. Some of this material is now displayed for the public to see and use, some of it is still awaiting the attention of an expert qualified to sort and file it, and unfortunately a great deal is still hidden away, neglected and unseen.

The numerous museums and libraries along the length and breadth of the nation vary from small local and municipal efforts, through regimental and Corps institutes, right up to the huge national museums. Nearly every one of them has some item of military interest on show or on file, and of course the regimental and national museums owe their very existence to promulgating military history. The main problem which most people experience as a result of all this wealth of information is that in a short space of time there is too much of it to take in. Therefore, this section is devoted to giving a few suggestions on how to make the best of museums and libraries as sources of information and research topics.

A few words are necessary regarding the types of museums involved—libraries will be dealt with later. As mentioned above there are many different types but the best ones to discuss first are the large national military museums. Top of this list must come the Imperial War Museum at Lambeth, in London. Housed in the building of the old Bethlehem mental hospital, the IWM is the home of what must be regarded as the finest collection of military relics from the years 1914-18 and 1939-45. It was established after 1918 as a permanent memorial to the events of the Great War, but the intervention of a second and more terrible conflict resulted in a further expansion to house the reminders of World War 2. Considering the limits imposed by the confines of what is a relatively small building the IWM can put on really excellent displays and exhibitions but its collection is so large that not all of it can be seen at any one time. Mention is made in another section of the vehicle and large item storage depot at Duxford but this is only rarely open for public examination. Even so, the IWM should be at the head of almost any list compiled by researchers.

The National Army Museum at Chelsea, again in London, is another important collection but it is devoted to the years up to 1914, after which the IWM is supposed to be the main authority. But in practice such neat definitions are not possible and the result is that some overlapping takes place, especially in the weapons' field so the Chelsea Museum, not too far from Lambeth, should be on the itinerary of many researchers. These two museums will probably suffice for the needs of most people but there are several other national collections, usually devoted to specialist topics, that can be consulted. The main snag with many of these is that they are not open to the general public for a variety of reasons. Some of them are necessarily housed or situated in areas or buildings occupied by the military or security-sensitive government departments. Examples are the Pattern Room at the Royal Small Arms Factory at Enfield Lock and the Infantry Weapons Museum in the School of Infantry at Warminster. For obvious reasons such establishments cannot be opened to the public at large as they are both working museums in the sense that they have been set up to educate and advise the establishments they are housed in. The same can be said of many regimental or Corps museums but thankfully many do open their doors to all-comers and their value cannot be overestimated.

There is one golden rule to be adhered to strictly when dealing with such 'enclosed' establishments and most regimental museums and that is to contact the curators or those responsible for their running well in advance of the date you wish to attend. If this simple precaution is taken even the most security-conscious establishment will do its best to help and assist you, often to the point of taking considerable trouble to show you what you need. But such assistance will not be given to mere gawpers—you must be able to establish in advance that you are a *bona fide* researcher or that you have good reason to gain access to such collections. A letter should be sent to the authority concerned outlining your reasons for wishing to gain access and the date and time you wish to attend. Discovering exactly who to contact is often no easy task and considerable letter-writing will be needed in some cases before you find the right person or department, so start your preparation for such visits well in advance. A book of this nature cannot give a list of addresses as it would be too long, and anyway many establishments cannot cater for the numbers of visitors which would result— they are already snowed-under with their day-to-day tasks.

To many readers the above precaution may seem so obvious that its inclusion is unnecessary, but ask almost any private museum authority how many times would-be visitors turn up without prior warning and expect to be shown round or given the run of a museum filled with weapons. Many of these establishments will probably be only too pleased to assist you in any number of ways, but if they refuse your request there is usually a very good reason. So don't be too disappointed, try somewhere else.

If you are permitted to enter one of the enclosed museums there are several more guidelines to follow. For a start, photography is usually out unless prior permission has been sought and given. At many establishments cameras are impounded as a matter of routine and anyone trying to get one past a security gate without letting the gate guardian know will soon find themselves in considerable trouble. To the layman such restrictions will seem petty and unnecessary but there are good reasons and the visitor must abide by the rules. Once inside the museum the general rule is stick with the guide and never try to enter a room or area without being conducted there. It is often very tempting to try and see what is 'round the corner' but if you attempt it you will soon be very unpopular and an escort off the premises is the very least you can expect. Again the rule to abide by is touch nothing unless you are invited to do so and at all times obey the guide. Once you have been conducted around you will frequently be asked to submit your findings or the results of your research to the authority concerned. To do so is an often-ignored courtesy anway, and your results should be submitted in full. Failure to carry out such a request can lead to all sorts of difficulties and it may mean that a future visit to that particular establishment will be ruled out.

Fortunately many museums are open to the general public and the confines and necessary restrictions of the enclosed establishment will not apply. This does not mean that anything goes. Nearly every museum has its own rules and regulations and the visitor must abide by them. For instance most museums ask visitors not to touch the exhibits but still priceless relics get handled to the point of destruction. Even when the public is invited to handle, approach or enter an exhibit care must be taken. Perhaps an extreme example could be quoted regarding the Tank Museum at Bovington in Dorset. There, visitors are allowed to climb over some of the tanks displayed but still the younger members of the public seem to regard the tanks as oversize climbing frames. Personally, I would prefer to see a tank covered with happy children rather than a squad of tank-killing infantry, but I wonder what the long-term effects of such treatment will be on some of the vehicles, even when they are built like tanks.

As a general rule smoking is not allowed, even when there are no prohibiting signs displayed in any particular area. Any visitor who does not stick to this rule and has insufficient self-control to cope with the temporary withdrawal from nicotine addiction will not have the necessary sticking-power of the dedicated researcher anyway!

Once inside a museum, all but the very smallest will usually present the researcher with a wide array of delectable items which scream out for examination and detailed perusal. This is where real researchers will stand out, for they should know exactly what it is they have come to see. A few minutes spent watching people entering the IWM will give an idea of what I mean. The casual visitor only wishing to see the sights will stand just inside the door wondering where to go first and will usually get distracted by the very first things he sees. The dedicated researcher will be seen to enter quickly and go direct to his particular section or item of interest. Once more we are back to our old topic of objectives. If you are visiting any museum you must be quite clear in your mind exactly what it is you wish to see, and once you are in you must adhere to that objective. In a place like the IWM temptations abound but you should only allow these to distract you once the main object of your visit has been achieved. Once again the importance of prior preparation will be seen to be all-important, but there will be occasions when you will visit a museum for the very first time and without any idea of what the collection contains.

I had an example of this myself recently while visiting Galway in Ireland. In the city centre I found a small city museum which I did not know existed, and thus had an opportunity to apply my own general ruling. Although the museum was very small I did not try to examine everything at one time but simply went around the museum as quickly as possible noting mentally what I wished to examine in detail for my second or third time around. I applied the same principle when I visited the National Museum in Dublin during my limited lunch breaks a short time later. In both cases I was able to note what there was to interest me particularly and return to later. In Galway I was thus able to examine closely an excellent little collection of Connaught Rangers cap badges. In Dublin I was able to study a really comprehensive collection of rifles, and some examples of the weapons used in 1916 and the 1922 Troubles. This technique of quick reconnaissance followed by a return to items noted is one I have developed over the years but others will no doubt have, or will acquire, their own methods.

A quick return to rules and regulations. The times we live in have produced their own extra restrictions and that often means that brief cases and hand bags are now examined on entry to a museum and in some cases they have to be handed in at the door for collection when you leave. The need for such precautions is self-evident but it may mean that, instead of taking a bulky note-pad to use for taking down information, you may have to make do with a small pocket-sized note book, so have one handy. As mentioned earlier, nearly every museum will prohibit the taking of photographs of items in their collections unless permission has been sought well in advance. Even then many authorities will prohibit the use of flash equipment which means that decent photographs will be impossible to take anyway. Thankfully this ruling is not universally applied—the above-mentioned Tank Museum at Bovington is a happy example—but it would be as well to enquire first.

When it comes to the actual examination of museum exhibits notes will usually have to be taken. This will often include sketching and detailed enlargements of small items and as this is a very variable skill each individual will have to set his own standards. Whatever the quality of such noting it is a good rule, and one that I have ignored to my cost, to head each sheet with a date and place at which it was made. In my own experience note-taking consists of making headings of important points or dates, with fine detail being taken only when really necessary. After a short length of time these notes have often been re-examined to locate a particular reference only to find that the sheets of original notes were in a jumbled mess, and important points lost in a welter of headings. Heading each sheet as suggested will prevent this happening. Some people find the use of small pocket tape-recorders of great assistance and I have taken one with me on many museum visits but I use them only when no one is around. I do this because I have found to my own cost that they can be very distracting for other people. Try reading a closely printed exhibit caption when someone is talking into a pocket tape-recorder on a totally different subject and you will soon see what I mean!

Libraries

The use of regimental and Corps institute libraries has been discussed in the section relating to the use of war diaries and other documents, but a few more words on the general techniques employed when using any library will be helpful.

Once again the Imperial War Museum at Lambeth gets a well-deserved mention for as well as being a first-class museum it also houses an enormous and magnificent library with books on just about every facet of warfare in the 20th Century. Unlike the museum section nearly all the library is housed in the IWM building itself but even today a warehouse has to be used to store a great pile of unsorted and unfiled documentation. Nevertheless, the range of material available in the IWM library is immense and likely to meet the needs of all but the most specialised researcher. But as with nearly every such reference library I know, the IWM is not open for the general public to walk in and out of at will. Access will only be granted after permission has been asked for well in advance by letter. As in the case of enclosed museums, the letter should contain your name, address, reason for wishing to use the library and, if possible, give a detailed list of the books you wish to examine. Also include the date you wish to attend. This applies to any library and not just to the IWM. The actual reading conditions will vary from library to library—some allow access to reading tables in the library proper, while others insist that separate reading rooms away from the bookshelves must be used.

If you are visiting the IWM library do not ask for too many books or files at any one time. The staff are most helpful but their good nature will start to wear thin if you ask for a pile of literature four-foot high. Needless to say the same thing goes for any library and it would be best to restrict your requests to a few well-chosen sources.

One department which the IWM does have that most other libraries lack is a photograph library. This is not housed in the main library, although it is in the same building, and if you wish to examine their central files prior permission must be asked for by a separate letter. If you do not have the particular serial number of the photograph you require (if you have, they can be ordered by post) it will mean that you will have to go through the albums held in the picture library, but you will not have to go through every one. If you have correctly itemised your particular interest or area the appropriate albums will be on a desk ready for you. Special order forms are available if you wish to have a copy for your own use. The printing costs are not prohibitive but a delay of some weeks must be expected before your order can be sent. A word of warning regarding these IWM photographs (and it usually applies to other photograph libraries). The prints are supplied for your use alone and they cannot be reproduced or published without permission of the Trustees of the IWM, and when they are published a reproduction fee will be exacted.

There are many other national libraries available to the researcher other than the IWM. For example, the British Museum Reading Room has just about any book, magazine or newspaper which has ever been published and access to them is open to all once they have gone through the proper channels and applied for a reader's ticket. The Public Records Office has a mass of material that can be scrutinised, again once the proper channels have been followed, but there are two restrictions which may prevent the novice from using their facilities to the full. One is that the correct serial number of the record file must be quoted in order for the staff to find it, and discovering this can be a major research task in its own right. The other restriction is that at the time of writing the bulk of the Public Records are in the process of being transferred from Chancery Lane in Central London to new and modern premises at Kew. During the period of the move some records will be unavoidably inaccessible.

When you get to the level of the regimental or Corps museum bear in mind a few extra factors. Many of the 'regimental' museums are often run on financial shoestrings as they are frequently part of a regimental or Corps institution that understandably directs the bulk of its limited income towards the upkeep of the widows, orphans and other dependants of the regiment. As a result many regimental and Corps libraries are housed in premises that are often far from adequate and with limited space and trained staff. From this it can be seen that in some cases their services are strictly limited, despite the wishes and inclinations of the staff concerned. Not every library has to restrict its activities in this way and an excellent example is the Royal Artillery Institution Library at Woolwich. I have always found the staff there most patient and understanding, and their library is first-class into the bargain. But bear in mind the limitations imposed by lack of space and facilities when approaching some of the smaller museums and limit your requests and enquiries accordingly.

This golden rule should be kept in mind when making enquiries by post. Every day just about any library you can think of gets a heap of letters containing requests of all kinds. These enquiries range from simple requests for access to read a certain file to letters that ask for information that will keep a trained researcher busy for months. Not surprisingly the latter enquiries rarely get very far, so if you are writing to any museum keep your letter and any requests as brief as possible—that way you will have far more chance of a favourable reply.

A few more, rather obvious, tips on behaviour in libraries generally. No matter in what location you are working keep your little area tidy and don't intrude into the space where others might be working. Don't make entries or notes in files or books without the librarian's permission. Such an act may be construed as vandalism but in some cases it might serve to indicate useful cross-references to others and it might expand or indicate misleading information to later readers. Don't start eating sandwiches or drinking tea from a flask in the middle of your researchings—and don't laugh, I have seen it happen. At all times keep your voice down to avoid distracting others working nearby, and as in museums the no smoking rule must apply. When you have finished your task, most libraries insist that only a member of the staff should replace the books or files in their places on the shelves, so leave them in a neat pile ready for removal.

Some of the larger libraries keep a photocopying machine for their own domestic use and in some cases its cost is supplemented by providing a copy service for visitors. If you choose to use such services remember that the library provides them for your convenience only and not so that rare or important manuscripts can be used by an individual for profit—the law of copyright still applies, and such copies are meant for your personal use only.

Outlined above are a few rules that I have discovered from my own experience. Obviously not all of them will apply to every case but if you stick to the broad sense of them you will not go very far wrong. Remember at all times when dealing with museums and libraries that you are the supplicant, not the master, and the objectives you will have set yourself will almost always be achieved.

Chapter 3

The use of models and sketches in research

Many people will have become interested in 20th Century military archaeology by way of modelling. One of the more remarkable phenomena of the last 20-odd years has been the huge and rapid growth of model making of all kinds, largely brought about by the growth in leisure time and the advent of the relatively cheap plastic kit. While many have been content just to build the models and place them on a shelf, equally as many have been intrigued and prompted into discovering more about the ships, aircraft or tanks they have made miniature replicas of. The problem with this activity is that very often the investigations grow into research of a more thorough nature and now many have got so involved with this that the modelling side has been virtually neglected. In my own case this has been true and I know of many other individuals who have found themselves in the same boat. While I spend my time investigating and researching for obscure facts the original kits and materials lie mouldering in my garden shed awaiting the day when I will get around to making them.

But as my work progresses I become more and more aware that modelling and its attendant skills are a great asset in many spheres of research, and this doesn't only apply to the well-trodden paths of AFV and aircraft history but also to some of the more obscure facets of our archaeology. In this chapter I will attempt to outline why this is so, but I have no intention of describing the techniques to be employed—each individual will have to work them out for himself. What I will do is give an outline of how modelling and sketching can be used to gain a better understanding of various aspects of modern warfare.

Modelling need not be an end in itself, but a medium towards greater comprehension of how something was built, why it was made in a certain fashion, and perhaps even why it was made at all. This rather pretentious statement can best be illustrated by a few examples. One of the best I can offer is shown by Ken Musgrave's drawing of a World War 1 9.2-inch howitzer and the accompanying photograph of a World War 2 mark. The 9.2 howitzer at first sight appears to be a formidable piece of aggressive mechanism, and in many ways it was, but for all its apparent complexity it was, in fact, a rather simple piece of gear structurally. But this will not be obvious until you start to look at it closely. When I say 'look at it' I do not mean literally, for to my knowledge none now exist, and we are forced to rely on photographs and, if possible, the original service manual.

To my knowledge Ken used only photographs for his drawing but alternatively he might have made a trip to the Royal Artillery memorial at Hyde Park Corner. But the main point is that when such investigations start you can begin to appreciate exactly why the weapon was constructed the way it was. To begin with, the howitzer was obviously not built for rapid movement and thus no means of moving it is included on the gun (ie, wheels, axles, etc). The barrel is fairly short which means it was intended for use fairly close to its target(s) and even a quick glance will reveal

Above *9.2-inch howitzer.* **Below** *Ken Musgrave's drawings of the same weapon.*

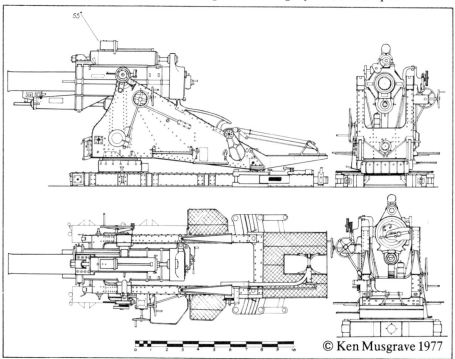

© Ken Musgrave 1977

that the cradle and its recoil and recuperator mechanism are fairly simple. The carriage, despite its size, is also quite basic and is only lengthened to the rear to enable the shell hoist and ramming gear to have an easy path to the breech. The traversing gear is large and bulky but again is reasonably simple.

Ken has gone to considerable trouble to draw in as much fine detail as possible, but if you now went on actually to build a model from his drawing you would find that it would be fairly easy to make and would result in only a few simple sub-assemblies. The photograph shows the Mark 2 version which had a longer barrel to give more range and a heavier recoil mechanism to cope with the bigger stresses involved. However, the photograph includes another interesting detail, namely the large box in front of the gun. A little investigation will reveal ᵗhat the box was filled with earth ballast to prevent the piece from heaving itself upwards off its platform when fired at high angles of elevation. The ballast had to be hand-loaded and dug out again before another move so once more the static conditions of the Western Front make themselves apparent.

So from a cursory look at an artillery piece we have learned quite a lot and the same can be said of anything else we might wish to study. AFV modellers have had a great deal of attention lavished on them to the extent that the younger generation is in danger of not gaining the depth of understanding which comes from detailed research—everything is handed to them on a plate. In fact, there are many other facets of our activity which still cry out for the modeller's and draughtman's attentions. Modern fortifications are one such important area. Anyone who has had even the briefest look at modern fortifications will no doubt have asked himself why such an odd-looking structure was built in such a strange location. Very often no official explanation will exist, or will be very difficult to find, so one solution is first to sketch a preliminary drawing and then to build a model. The model need not be very exact or very grand but as you build it and refer back to your original sketch all sorts of details will reveal themselves. You will see that the odd-shaped approach route is hidden from a possible flanking position. An overhanging roof gives overhead protection from fire or aerial attack, but at the same time permits observations of a target to be made. The room at the back with no apparent function will be seen to be a bomb-proof store for water or the like. Build up the outside of your structural model with plaster of Paris using the local contours as a guide and you will soon see how extra protection and camouflage aided its defence. The possibilities are legion—perhaps the roof could be made to lift to expose the interior; or an attempt could be made to discover the layout of internal equipment; or long-removed ventilation trunking could be built into a model to reveal internal space limitations, and so forth.

While modelling can show such internal features, external factors such as siting can usually only be sorted out by sketching. Both pillboxes and coastal defences were often situated in some very odd locations but the military mind is not so daft as some would assume and such expensive items as concrete defences were usually positioned for very good reasons. Today such reasons may be obscure but the use of a contour map will often reveal the answer. For example take a stretch of coastline which has several defence positions. On a map try drawing in their exact locations and visit each one to determine their limits of observation and fire—if possible enter the structures and observe these limits. However, you must bear in mind that fire limits were frequently less than those for observation, and remember the limits of elevation or depression as well. Sketch these on to your map and you will be surprised how the various arcs interlock and cover each other. Don't just do this horizontally; try vertical cross-sections as well. This simple practice can be very instructive especially where really odd features can be found. In one part of Jersey a single anti-tank gun mounting is still to be seen in apparent splendid isolation in a thicket. Investigation and a little sketching on a map soon revealed that it was originally on a 360° traverse turntable and covered a re-entrant along with another fire position further away across a small valley. The thicket quite simply wasn't there when the positions were first built.

Modelling and sketching have many uses in our field of interest—I have mentioned but a few. However, in almost every sphere of our activity some application will be found for both. You may note that I have made no mention of the degree of skills that are needed, and neither have I mentioned techniques but this is deliberate as this section is only meant to give ideas, not details.

Chapter 4

Military architecture

The term military architecture has been chosen for this section despite the fact that it is not really the term which should be used. Many of the structures which will be described below are the very antithesis of what architecture is generally held to be since they are nearly all strictly functional in their sparse utility and normally, if they have any aspect which is pleasing to behold, it is very much an unsought-for by-product of the process which created them. The field described below is a wide one and although it will cover mainly structures, sometimes other features will be mentioned.

The years since 1900 have seen some drastic innovations but military architecture has seen only a revision of constructional methods and layout rather than any violent change of function. Originally military architecture was mainly concerned with various forms of protection against a mobile enemy and modern military architecture is still concerned with that role. The main difference is that, in years gone by the weapons against which military architecture was supposed to afford protection were puny when compared to the tremendous destructive power of modern aggressive machinery. This fact alone explains why, in comparison with an era when castles and forts stood out clear against a skyline, modern military architecture is often difficult to see as most of it has been buried beneath the protective surface. When modern military structures have to be constructed above ground they are often massive edifices fabricated from concrete and steel.

Concrete and steel are usually the dominant materials encountered in modern military architecture, but of the two, concrete predominates. Its use has become widespread for several reasons, not the least of which are the measure of protection it can afford against high explosives and the relative speed and ease with which it can be used. Concrete began to be used for fortifications around the turn of the century and from then onwards its use spread until, by 1939, it had virtually replaced masonry in military structures. By this date its strength and usefulness had been greatly increased by reinforcing techniques such as the use of steel rods and girders. Also the gradual increase in high explosive efficiency had meant that the thicknesses of concrete had grown to massive proportions to give protection above ground. Below ground these thicknesses need not be so great for earth can often serve as a protection by itself—consequently many military structures went underground. Perhaps the best example of this prior to 1939 was the French Maginot Line. After 1940 the Germans followed the same principles to construct much of the Atlantic Wall.

Military architecture is not purely defensive in its functions. The term can be used to cover all the multifarious needs of modern armies. But once away from the purely 'battle' aspects of military structures one encounters their other feature—impermanence. In the 20th Century the very scale of the conflicts involved the use of masses of men and women in such huge numbers that time-honoured building

The magnificent fire control tower at Les Landes seen through the outline of a wrecked entrance to another observation post nearby. This tower is one of the author's favourite structures.

The interior of a typical German gun bunker. Wherever possible these bunkers were built into headlands and nearby hills and valleys to give increased protection. As can be seen from the stove in the foreground, heating and ventilation were provided in case of a prolonged siege.

methods could no longer be employed. In times gone by such mundane items as barracks and stores were built from materials and at a pace which differed little from normal civilian practices. From 1914 onwards that was no longer possible. Accommodation and storage suddenly had to be provided for thousands upon thousands and the supplies of billets and canvas accommodation were soon outstripped. The use of prefabricated and lightly constructed buildings became commonplace and the Weblee, Tarrant and Nissen huts became part of the military scene. The light and hurried construction of these buildings meant that very few of them survived after 1919, but 1939 and the years after saw a still more vast explosion of temporary structures for an even greater variety of purposes. Perhaps the most well-known of these buildings was the Nissen Hut which dated from World War 1— many of them are still with us today. But of all the thousands of huts, stores, garages, workshops and camps which were hurriedly assembled in the two World Wars, very few now remain. All that can be found of many of them are their concrete bases and the traces of the roads that served them. Only where the temporary buildings were found to have a peacetime or civilian use have any survived. All too often huge areas which were once military towns with thousands of prefabricated buildings are now derelict stretches of overgrown waste ground with nothing left standing.

But this does not mean that there is nothing for the modern military archaeologist to see or discover. All over the United Kingdom there are remains of gun sites, camps, coastal batteries, depots, prisoner-of-war camps, magazines and all the other relics of a nation at war. In Europe the same picture is repeated but there even more can be seen and discovered. The remains of the Maginot Line and the Atlantic Wall will be with us for hundreds of years yet, and it seems unlikely that anyone will ever bother to dismantle the U-boat pens at Brest.

In the United Kingdom one particular area which will always attract the military archaeologist is the Channel Islands. The number and variety of military structures built by the Germans during their occupation of the islands between 1940 and 1945 was great and many of them can still be seen and examined today. Many of the military sites are positioned in some of the most spectacular scenery the islands have to offer and the temptation to combine a holiday with investigating some of the sites has been too much for me several times in the past. Even the less adventurous holiday-maker cannot escape the German military presence for, whilst lazing on the beaches in front of what they take to be normal sea defences, they are in fact lying before German-constructed anti-tank walls (*Panzermauern*), and in some places people now take tea in what were gun casemates or control bunkers. Perhaps the most spectacular structures are the fire control towers which can be found ail around the Channel Islands and, indeed, are peculiar to them. Many of these multi-storied towers, with their characteristic wide vision slots for fire control instruments and rangefinders, are open to the public but one of them, at Noirmont Point, has now been taken over by the CIOS and thus has a better chance of preservation than some of the others. Despite their sturdy construction many of the others will succumb in

One of the most imposing of all the Channel Island towers is that at L'Angle on Guernsey. Despite its aggressive appearance, it was never used (Colin Partridge).

Above *Inside one of the control rooms of the Noirmont post taken over by the CIOS in Jersey (Michael Ginns).*

Left *A small detail of just part of the wiring and communication gear still installed, or being installed, in the Noirmont control post.*

time to the elements, and already a few have collapsed as cliffs have eroded beneath them. For me these towers are some of the most interesting and visually appealing buildings I have ever seen. Perched on the edge of massive cliffs with their silent slots peering out to sea, they create an aura and sense of their period which no other relic of warfare has, for me, been able to evoke.

But the towers are not the only sights that the Channel Islands have to offer. All the islands have coastal gun sites, control bunkers, gun positions, beach defences and all the defensive features of modern warfare. Perhaps the main appeal of the islands is that such a wide variety of structures can be seen within a relatively small space. Of the two main islands Jersey has the greater variety but Guernsey has the greatest concentration and has the added attraction, for me again, of the site of the *Mirus* battery. The military archaeology novice could do a great deal worse than take an exploratory holiday in the Channel Islands. Not only will he or she have a very pleasant and interesting time but some idea will be formed of what to look for on returning home. For the simple fact is that in the United Kingdom (and elsewhere) it is sometimes very difficult to determine exactly what the function of a half-buried or hidden concrete structure was.

The ability to recognise the function of a piece of military architecture is a most useful accomplishment for the novice archaeologist. To the uninitiated the sight of an open-sided concrete box will mean little but to someone who has done even a little investigation it will indicate a 'ready-ammunition' magazine and will thus mean that the area was the site of a coastal battery (or, if inland, an anti-aircraft gun site). Nearly everyone can recognise the common or garden (literally) pillbox and for several reasons it is given its own section elsewhere, but recognition of other military features is not always easy. For example, the military depot or munitions dump is not always easy to spot. Some of them are still in use today and are thus easy to see but many, from both wars, are now simply marked on the ground by a railway spur or road leading to nowhere and petering out in the middle of a large flat expanse.

The sites of military dumps and depots from World War 1 are now few and far between. The reasons for this are not that there weren't many, for there were, but simply because World War 1 was mainly fought in France and it was there that the great bulk of the British Army's depots were built up. Another reason for the dearth of depots from that era is that the majority were only meant to be temporary and the buildings associated with them were constructed accordingly. But World War 2 imposed a new situation. Starting in 1939 the British Army once more began to build up a series of depots in France but by mid-1940 they were back in the United Kingdom. From then onwards the crowded British islands became even more crowded, not only with the multifarious sites, training camps, depots and stores of an expanding army, but gradually with the same appendages of numerous Allied armies. The whole of the United Kingdom became one massive armed camp and by 1944 there were few parts of Britain where the sight of uniforms and the sounds of vehicles or weapons in training (or anger) were far away. The British Forces were everywhere but other nationalities were usually alloted to single areas or regions. American troops were first stationed all along the South Coast and the adjacent counties but in time their numbers grew until they were also stationed in Wales and Cheshire—more were in Northern Ireland. Canadian troops planted their administrative roots in Kent and Sussex while the large number of Poles fighting with the Allies were mainly stationed in Scotland. Other smaller contingents were scattered in various parts of Britain. There were Dutch troops in Wolverhampton and Belgians in Birmingham (and more in Northern Ireland). There were small enclaves of Allied troops and their associated camps and depots all around Britain and a study of such 'visitors' in local areas can be a study in itself. Very often there were overlaps and anomalies but they can only add to the interest of such an investigation.

Apart from such sites as depots, most parts of the United Kingdom had anti-aircraft gun sites. Where possible these were sited in flat open vicinities and very often they were furnished with concrete protection and magazines, and pre-fabricated accommodation. On the coasts more gun sites were placed for local or coastal defence and in some cases these doubled as anti-aircraft guns as well. Some of these gun sites covered quite a large area for not only were there the guns (usually situated in clusters of four) but there had to be concrete cover for radar vehicles and their users. More cover had to be given to magazines for the ammunition expenditure of even a single battery was at times prodigious. The control centre was another candidate for concrete protection as was the communication centre (which might boast radio in addition to the more usual land lines). The rest of the site usually had temporary accommodation not only for the personnel but also for the numerous vehicles which most batteries accumulated.

All along the Atlantic Wall old tank turrets, usually left over when tanks were converted to assault or mobile field artillery vehicles, were emplaced to 'beef-up' local defence posts. This example is a French R-35 turret still with its gun fitted and emplaced in the grounds of Elizabeth Castle, Jersey.

After the war many of the anti-aircraft gun sites were demolished but a large number still remain, along with their associated searchlight sites.

The coastal gun sites were very much on the same scale as the anti-aircraft gun sites but there were many variations depending on the role of the battery and its position. The largest of the coastal sites were used for the long-range batteries such as those at Dover which were used to shell shipping in the Channel—these were the true coastal artillery batteries. Lower down the scale were the smaller calibre batteries which could engage shipping but were primarily local defence units. Right at the small calibre level were the beach defence batteries, often with only one or two guns, and the harbour defence batteries. A listing of all the coastal batteries in the United Kingdom is given in an appendix at the back of this book. In most instances the batteries mentioned had only one or two small calibre guns and in many cases very little remains to be seen of them today. But in other locations there will be not only tangible remains but a great deal of information which will form the basis for a research project.

Associated with the beach defence batteries were numerous beach obstacles erected or placed on the most likely landing beaches along the South Coast. These obstacles varied a great deal from arrangements of scaffolding poles to the concrete blocks used inland. Some of them were erected underwater to hinder the approach of landing barges while others were placed on the beaches themselves to provide obstacles to tanks. In most cases these obstacles were cleared soon after 1945 but even now the remains of a few stretches of these relics of 1940 can still be seen, usually in places which are rarely visited. One example I know of is on the Chesil Bank near Abbottsbury where an extensive line of anti-tank obstacles (covered by a few pillboxes) can still be seen snaking their way across the shingle. Another, and more unusual, example can be found on the beach at Climping, near Littlehampton. Here twisted scaffolding poles can still be found which are remnants of 1940 anti-invasion underwater obstacles.

A prominent feature of the war of 1939 to 1945 was the air raid shelter, built for the services and for the use of the civilian population. In the larger cities large numbers of brick and concrete shelters were built in parks, open spaces and even in the streets themselves. In less populated areas personal shelters were issued to individual households and in such situations the air raid shelter became an accepted part of social life. The most familiar of the individual shelters was the Anderson, a small simple construction fabricated from corrugated iron sheets. They sprang up in back gardens by the thousand and many were improved by covering them with earth or brick. Many still remain as they had become so much a part of the scene that people decided to leave them where they were 'just in case', and in the meantime large numbers have been pressed into service as garden tool stores or coal bunkers. The larger public shelters did not survive so well. Many lingered on for several years after 1945 but by now nearly all have gone apart from a few which have been pressed into such public service functions as telephone exchanges and the like. But in some of our larger cities you can still see the odd fading public shelter signs painted in various out-of-the-way places.

Out in the country you can still occasionally come across the odd weapon pit, usually lined with concrete or steel. Many of them are still situated at crossroads or at other prominent points and evidence of concrete or steel obstacles can often be found nearby. These weapon pits had a range of functions. Sometimes they were built to guard tented encampments which left little other evidence of their presence, and sometimes they were built to cover road blocks or important road junctions. Most of them were just lined holes in the ground but some had a small measure of overhead protection and were furnished with more than just the guard's rifle or light machine-gun. One of the more wide spread weapons in use in 1940 and 1941 was the Blacker Bombard, a spigot mortar which was supposed to have an anti-tank capability. Other such extemporised weapons in use in those days were the Northover Projector, a simple gun which fired glass anti-tank projectiles, and the Smith Gun, another very simple 'pipe gun'. Such weapons saw very little use other than with the Home Guard but they form a subject for research in their own right.

Other structures which sprang up all over the United Kingdom included not only

Just as intriguing as many military structures are the old signs that can still frequently be seen. This sign was on a light AA gun pit wall and was used as a rough orientation point for laying and reporting.

training and accommodation camps but also prisoner-of-war camps. In both wars large numbers of POWs were used as farm labourers in the United Kingdom but during World War 2 most of the prisoners so used were Italians—the majority of the Germans were sent to camps in Canada. As with so many other types of camp, the POWs were housed in accommodation which was meant to be only temporary and subsequently many were rapidly removed after 1945. But here and there some of the these camps still remain. In many places they are overgrown and derelict but in other locations the buildings are still being put to use. One Italian camp near where I live is still in use as a riding stable. Camps from World War 1 are now rare. I know of the site of only one. That is above St Ouens Bay in Jersey where the concrete foundation blocks of a 1914-1918 German POW camp can still be seen—today the site is used as a picnic area.

The United Kingdom still has numerous sites with a multitude of purposes which can still be seen. Almost every locality has some relic or another from one or both major wars somewhere to be examined and a book of this nature cannot cover them all. What each researcher must do is discover exactly what remains in his or her particular area and make a determined effort to record what is left. If possible the site should be visited but do take care to obtain permission to gain access if the site is in private hands. These islands of ours are so crowded that what appears to be derelict land is often privately owned and many people, understandably, take umbrage at others tramping over their property. Often a site may be found to be in local authority or public ownership but again, permission must be obtained before you try to move in.

With the formalities cleared the task of recording can commence. Photography and sketching are the two main recording media in use but whichever is used the best results obtainable should be aimed at. If photography is used a degree of clearing away undergrowth and rubbish is often necessary to obtain useful results but don't forget that for recording purposes some form of scaling reference is needed. A measuring ruler or something similar in the picture frame is often all that is wanted. Sketches with dimensions are often more effective than photographs on some sites, especially where large areas have to be covered, but as you go take as many measurements as possible. Ideally a properly detailed drawing should be made of each site but many people shirk from this task as they think they lack the necessary skills. However, most modern military sites are strictly functional and stick to straight lines and right-angle corners so drawing plans is usually no particularly difficult task. A good idea is to draw up any preliminary plans on graph paper and afterwards trace out the finished product. Ink should be used for the final drawing with as many dimensions entered as possible and on each sheet there should be a mention of the precise area covered by that drawing and the date when the information was gathered. When finished the drawings should not be just hidden away and forgotten for they will be a valuable archive for the future. A copy of your work should be presented to the local authority or local museum. Mention of your local museum prompts me to mention that very often they can be invaluable mines of information on the locality and their assistance is frequently important.

As mentioned above almost every part of the United Kingdom has a few relics of two major wars but some areas are richer in remains than others. Dover is an obvious example. The Channel Islands are of particular interest as mentioned above and the Portsmouth region is another area of great interest—the main problem there is that many of the most interesting sites are still used by the services. In the West Country there are many relics to be seen around Plymouth and the surrounding area. East Anglia is another happy hunting-ground for the military archaeologist while further north the Humber and the Tees are rich in relics, especially coastal batteries.

In Europe the remains of Hitler's Atlantic Wall continue to suprise and amaze the investigator, not only for their scope and degree of preservation but by their sheer scale. All along the coasts of France the massive remains of gun emplacements, control and communication bunkers and batteries still stand guard over some of the wildest coastlines in Europe. A journey along almost any sector of the French Channel coast will reveal concrete monoliths pushing their way through the sand dunes while inland the remains of V1 launching sites can still be found hidden away in woods and odd stretches of waste ground. For me one of the most interesting sites is that at Mimoyeques in the Pas de Calais. Hidden away beneath a hill are the sealed remains of 'Millipede', a multi-barrelled 15 cm gun that was meant to be Hitler's V-3, the gun that was built to bombard London. The guns were damaged in an air raid in 1944 and were never finished—the remains were sealed by demolitions carried out by Canadian engineers in 1945. One day those sealed remains will be uncovered for future generations to wonder at.

Elsewhere in France the Maginot Line can still be seen, usually hidden away in some of the wildest forests in Western Europe. Many of the larger Line forts are virtually invisible above ground but here and there the odd turret or entrance can be found. But a word of warning is necessary regarding the Maginot Line. Many of the wilder stretches have been left virtually untouched since 1945 and as a result there are still stretches where minefields remain uncleared. The obvious moral is to avoid wandering from the defined paths or roads. Another warning is that some of the old forts are still used by the French services for a variety of purposes, including the nerve centres of the *Force de Frappe*. Anyone who has ever had anything to do with the French methods of security should realise those areas are definitely ones to avoid.

Another part of France which still has a great attraction to the British visitor in any capacity is the World War 1 battlefields. They are really a subject of research in their own right and over the years a great deal of effort has been lavished on them. Today they are places of pilgrimage where ranks upon ranks of graves can be seen on

The author gives scale to one of the 22 cm gun pits near Les Landes, Jersey. The large firing platform, although a bit rusty, could soon be made fit for its original purpose.

A beach defence gun, actually a French 105 mm gun taken from the Maginot Line defences, at St Catherines, on Jersey. Originally the gun was camouflaged and the concrete was lined with timber but after 1945 timber was in great demand as fuel and nearly every structure in the Channel Islands has been stripped of its original timber facings.

or near every major battlefield. Here and there stretches of the old front-line trenches are preserved, some very artificially (the hideous *Tranchée du Baionettes* at Verdun is one unpleasant example), but other sectors such as the Canadian memorial at Vimy have been left almost in their original 1918 state. Visiting the Great War battlefields is a sobering and often humbling experience. The sight of all those beautifully-kept cemeteries and imposing memorials is something which cannot fail to impress even the most cynical and hardened soul, and the sound of the Last Post being played, as it still is played every evening, under the Menin Gate is one of the most plaintive sounds anyone will ever hear.

But pilgrimage apart there is still much to discover of the Great War battlefields, even after nearly 60 years. Away from the cemeteries and monuments the old front lines are now nearly all returned to their original purposes. Here and there odd stretches of trench can be found with mouldering relics of military occupation still in situ. But it must be emphasised right away that searching for such relics is a very dangerous activity. So much lethal hardware was delivered to the old front lines that some of it is still hidden there and even now almost every week results in yet another cache of dangerous debris being uncovered and very often deaths or injuries result from shells or mines being accidentally discovered. Even human remains are still being found. The result of all this high explosive and uncovered corpses is that in many places the soil itself is highly poisonous and any small cut or graze can result in very nasty wounds that take some time to heal. Notwithstanding such hazards there are many people who would argue that searching for relics is in itself something of a form of desecration and the author himself must side with those who put forward this argument. All too often the search for relics of the Great War has been reduced to mere souvenir-hunting. Bearing in mind the risk of personal injury and the risk of desecration of human remains one can only wonder if the game is worth the candle. But at the same time it must be said that I, for one, have seen very few accurate sketches or layouts of trench systems and pillbox layouts as used on the Western

Front. One is thus impressed with the need for someone to carry out a survey of what still remains in France and record what little there is left. Doubtless the information has been recorded somewhere but I have yet to find it.

The novice who has an interest in the French battlefields (and there can be few military archaeologists who have none) could do a lot worse than carry out a preliminary recce by going on one of the battlefield tours which are laid on by several tour operators—usually by coach although I have heard of one firm which organises hiking tours. Such a tour will give anyone an idea of what there is to see and the scale of the country they will have to cover. After that more trips will have to be made accurately to cover any particular sectors of interest. But I have to repeat that the World War 1 battlefields are a study in themselves and well outside the confines of this book.

Further reading

A topic like military architecture cannot be usefully dealt with in just a few lines, which is all this book can devote to the subject. Further reading is necessary just to get a basic grasp of the subject and a listing is given below of books which I have found very useful. It is not meant to be fully comprehensive but once the following works have been examined each individual will be guided by them along the paths they wish to follow.

Close to the top of any list compiled by anyone with an interest in military architecture must be *Architecture of Aggression*, by Keith Mallory and Arvid Ottar. Despite its rather misleading title (the architecture described is almost all concerned with defence, not aggression) this work contains the best résumé of the numerous types of structure thrown up during two World Wars. It contains many illustrations and gives many examples of drawings and photographs that tyros would do well to follow.

Anyone who wishes to investigate modern military architecture must be able to put it into a proper historical context and two books can help anyone do this very

The thick steel observation cupola used by the Naval battery at Noirmont on Jersey. The control rooms below this cupola form part of the control post taken over by the Jersey Branch of the CIOS.

well. The first is *Fortress*, by Ian Hogg, and the other *Military Architecture* by Quentin Hughes. Both are well-written and illustrated works which give a very good background to their subject.

As most readers of this book will concern themselves with the military legacy of the United Kingdom they virtually have a duty to read Basil Collier's excellent history *The Defence of the United Kingdom*, published in the first-class HMSO 'History of the Second World War' series. Packed with maps, photographs and tables this book is a *must* for anyone with an interest in the period. Unfortunately it is now difficult to obtain and recourse may have to be made to public libraries.

From here on more specialised works need to be consulted. Anyone interested in coastal batteries should consult *The History of Coast Artillery in the British Army*, by Colonel Maurice-Jones, or *Coast Defences of England and Wales 1856-1956*, again by Ian Hogg. Both are excellent works. For those investigating the activities of the British anti-aircraft arm, at the time of writing there is still nothing better than General Sir Frederick Pile's *Ack-Ack*. It was first published in 1949 but there is still nothing to replace it.

Further afield, the defences of Jersey built by the Germans are well described in a little book entitled *German Fortifications in Jersey*, written by two good friends of mine, Michael Ginns and Peter Bryans. I have no hesitation in recommending this book to anyone who visits the island. To add to its attraction it costs only £1 and is available from 'Rangistacey', Rue des Sablons, Grouville, Jersey.

Another publication privately produced in the Channel Islands is *Hitler's Atlantic Wall*, written by another friend, Colin Partridge. Its title is self-explanatory and its contents and presentation are first-class. Again the drawings and plans provide an excellent guide to what the novice should strive towards. The quality of the contents can be judged by the fact that the author has been along all the various sections of the wall and is well qualified to write such a book as he himself is an architect. The book can be obtained from DI Publications, Rue des Goddards, Castel, Guernsey. Price £3.50.

Anyone wishing to visit the battlefields of World War 1 in France must take with them one of the best guides to the area now available, namely *Before Endeavours Fade*, by Rose E.B. Coombs. This book is superbly illustrated and outlines guided tours to just about every part of the Western Front. By itself it is worth having even if you can never get to France. Priced at only £2.50 it is excellent value and a book well worth having.

A typical Panzermauern anti-tank wall of the type to be found all along the Atlantic Wall. As can be seen this section was never fully completed.

Chapter 5

The pillbox

The military structures which are now generally known as 'pillboxes' had their tentative origins during the Russo-Japanese War of 1905. They came into really large-scale use during World War 1 when they sprang up wherever time was allowed for one side or the other to build organised static defences. Their proliferation during that conflict was due to their extremely strong concrete or masonry construction and the fact that their small loopholes could be so arranged that a relatively small number of trained men and weapons could command a wide field of fire. The pillbox coupled with the machine-gun made a formidable obstacle which could rarely be bypassed in an attack without a great deal of diversionary effort, and at times in 1917 and 1918 a single German pillbox manned by a few men with one or two machine-guns was often able to hold up the advance of whole battalions of infantry. Observers of the efficiency of these small and relatively cheap structures were not slow to note their value, and their use spread. By the end of 1918 many pillboxes had been incorporated into British coast defence lines, especially along the East Coast, with concentrations in East Anglia and around the mouth of the Thames. In some places, a few of these World War 1 pillboxes can still be seen and several of them were in use between 1939 and 1945.

But it was the years 1940 and 1941 which saw the rapid growth of pillboxes in the United Kingdom. When France and the Low Countries fell in May and June 1940 Great Britain was seen to be in imminent danger of invasion and hurried defence measures were taken. The pillbox featured prominently in the counter-invasion defence plans for the same reasons that were to the fore between 1914 and 1918. They were cheap, relatively easy to build and each one required less than a platoon to man it, plus a few weapons. In 1940 and 1941 men and weapons were in very short

An almost 'standard' coastal pillbox, SZ 209931 PCS.

SZ 018997 PCW. A pillbox still with its original corrugated iron camouflage to make it resemble an ordinary shed, and still with concrete anti-tank blocks in the foreground.

supply so gradually systems of defence lines anchored on clusters of pillboxes were built all around the British coasts with the main concentrations on the south and east coasts. The first structures built in 1940 were often on, or very near, the likely invasion beaches. Some of the early pillboxes were very simple affairs built from local masonry or brick and many were hurriedly camouflaged with shingle or sand— very few of these early efforts now remain which is not surprising as they were intended to be only temporary. As time allowed they were replaced with what has now become recognised as the standard pillbox shape, namely a flat-sided and roofed hexagonal single-storey structure constructed from reinforced concrete or a mixture of brick and concrete. Five of the six walls usually had a weapon embrasure with a protected entrance at the rear, but some had all-round fire embrasures with a concealed entrance and others were reached by a protecting short tunnel. Variations were legion. Some were simply slab-sided four-walled affairs, others had only three sides, and some asymmetric shapes were built to suit local conditions or locations.

At the same time as the coast defence pillboxes were being hurriedly built, a second line of extended defences was being constructed inland to form what was known as the GHQ Line. This was to have been the main defence line against any attacking forces and as such was a much more carefully sited line than the coast defences which had to be emplaced wherever there seemed to be a likely invasion point. The GHQ Line was able to take account and make use of any natural approach obstacle or feature and the pillbox was used, either singly or in mutually-supporting clusters, to defend these points. Although each pillbox, or pillbox cluster, commanded only a small stretch of country, they gradually stretched in a line across Southern England to the North of Yorkshire. Many pillboxes were well-camouflaged and emplaced to command a wide field of fire but in some cases their hurried construction meant that they were painfully exposed and visible, although camouflage helped to reduce their visibility. This camouflage often reached ingenious levels, especially with some of the coastal pillboxes which were disguised as beach kiosks or even roundabouts. Inland some were disguised as garden sheds or were covered in turf or shrubbery. As time and resources allowed the pillboxes were made into even better obstacles by the use of concrete blocks in various shapes. These were placed along fields of fire covered by the 'parent' pillbox and they were intended to impede the transit of tanks or vehicles. If roads were involved road blocks which could be easily placed in position were fashioned from steel posts embedded in yet more concrete. The concrete blocks took several forms. Perhaps the most well-known were 'Pimples', often wrongly called 'Dragons' Teeth', which were semi-pyramids that were virtually impassable for tanks. Simpler obstacles were self-explanatory 'Blocks', and 'Coffins' which were simply extended blocks. These concrete obstacles are often all that remain of some very extensive defence systems.

About 15,000 pillboxes were constructed in the United Kingdom between 1940 and 1945, the bulk of them being built in 1940 and 1941. Not all were in the beach defences or the GHQ Line for many others were built in positions for purely local defence. Likely locations for these were the entrances to railway tunnels, by railway bridges, at the entrances to important factories, or by river and canal crossings. Some were emplaced in positions which seemed to offer good fields of fire alone and there were few parts of the United Kingdom that did not have at least one pillbox somewhere in the locality.

At first the pillboxes were manned by the Army and in some cases by the Royal Air Force (especially on airfields), or by the Royal Navy or Royal Marines. Gradually they were handed over to the Local Defence Volunteers, later known as the Home Guard. In many cases the weapons involved were simply rifles but machine-guns gradually increased in number and eventually anti-tank guns (other than crude Home Guard contrivances) were emplaced at some selected points. These anti-tank guns, usually 2 prs, were accorded special pillboxes of rectangular construction and with larger embrasures than normal, but more often the sole anti-tank defences were provided by anti-tank rifles and grenades. The latter tended to negate the

SU 138373 PCW. A pillbox that was originally emplaced to defend the old High Post airfield.

SU 923561 PC36. A typical all-round defence pillbox. Many of this type used a concealed sunken entrance.

purpose of the pillbox as such close-quarter weapons meant the defenders had to leave their protective cover.

With the take-over by the Home Guard the local pillbox often became very much a local centre of war effort, and most were equipped with all the comforts of home. But once the war was over they were usually stripped of anything which might be considered useful, and the wooden camouflage superstructures were often used as fuel during the severe winters of 1946 and 1947, so that in a very short space of time many became derelict shells. Not long after 1945 many were demolished as they were emplaced in awkward positions for normal civilian commerce, but in many country areas landowners with a pillbox on their property were offered a sum of money, usually about £10, to let the pillboxes remain where they were rather than have the civil authorities bother about removing them. In many cases the money was accepted. But of the 15,000 or so built during the war only around 4,000 now remain.

The figure of 4,000 has been reached by the calculations and efforts of a Mr H. Wills who lives near Salisbury in Wiltshire—a good pillbox county. Over a period of years he has amassed a great deal of information regarding the common pillbox and he has also gradually made a census of those remaining. The way he has done this is worthy of study as it provides a very good example of how military archaeology should be approached and carried out.

Mr Wills' interest in the pillbox was aroused by the fact that very often they are the sole tangible relics of the momentous years of 1940 and 1941 which still survive in most localities. During those years the nation was in danger of imminent invasion and the whole population stood to and suffered the privations of air raids and separation from loved ones and friends. With a gradual lessening of the danger of German invasion much of the spirit and aura of those desperate days gradually ebbed away so that now it is difficult for new generations to realise the spirit of the period. Many people would have it remain so but there are others who feel that some form of local memorial should remain to those historically important times (the local war memorial to the dead is really in a separate category). With this in mind Mr Wills became painfully aware that in many cases the pillboxes which remain are all there is to show for those years and he also became aware that many are still being

SU 102314. Anti-tank obstacles near Wilton, emplaced to cover a river crossing.

PILLBOX AND DEFENCE SURVEY						From
	**P**lease fill in details as follows: DATE:Visited/Seen POSITION: OS Sheet No. and National Grid Reference TYPE: Polygonal, rectangular, circular, special design CONSTRUCTION: Concrete, brick or mixt re DIRECTION which pillbox faces— ent ar.ce usually at rear SPECIAL FEATURES, e.g. Disguised as Summer House
						Do/do not send me another card.
Date	OS No.	Grid Ref.	Type	Construction	Direction	Special Features
	THANK YOU for your help— Post costs prevent additional ackr.owledgment.

Henry Wills' census card.

demolished for very little reason other than that they were considered to be eyesores by the local authorities or that they stood in the way of some building or road development. Thus he started on a course of action to try and bring the pillbox to public notice.

To this end he has embarked on a series of exercises to prevent the demolition of important pillboxes with unusual features or roles. He has been successful in some cases in obtaining local preservation orders to ensure future generations will have some idea of the desperate measures taken in 1940 and 1941. But perhaps the most important historical task Mr Wills will have carried out is his census of remaining pillboxes. By gradually spreading his message through the media, including letters to local papers and specialist magazines, and even via radio and television, Mr Wills has compiled an invaluable record of one aspect of Britain's defences which (hopefully) will not be necessary again. The basis of his census is a simple postcard which can be seen in the accompanying illustration. This self-addressed card is sent to any contact willing to help and it covers the main points that need to be recorded regarding each remaining pillbox.

The first of these points is exactly where a pillbox is (not forgetting the date the information was collected). For this purpose the National Grid system is used. The Grid Letters precede the actual Grid Reference, which should be given to at least six figures—more if your map reading is up to it. The Grid Letters can be found on the margin of any Ordnance Survey map. The Grid Reference is given in the conventional manner, ie, the grid square and segment from east to west and then the grid square and segment from south to north ('into the house and up the stairs')—but don't forget the Grid Letters. For a typical example, a pillbox in Portsmouth Dockyard would be given the map reference SU627003 and the same reference is also given to any sketches or photographs associated with that pillbox. It is also useful to note the type, eg, hexagonal, square, etc, and the construction. Construction will usually be concrete or brick or a mixture of the two. The direction in which the pillbox faces should also be noted. This may not always be obvious but

SZ 033787 DCSE. A typical conversion of a gun emplacement. It is now used as a shelter. This example is at Swanage.

bear in mind that the entrance was usually at the rear—the point of the compass is what is wanted here. Any special features such as the remains of camouflage should be noted and if it possible to get inside the pillbox, the pillbox designation should be recorded—this is usually found marked over the inside of the entrance door.

Mr Wills is always pleased to obtain any information on surviving pillboxes, even to the extent of duplicating his present findings. He is still anxious to improve his coverage of the Yorkshire and Lincolnshire areas and would welcome any locations, sketches, photographs, etc, as outlined above. The end product of all this research and effort will be a compiled record to be presented to the Imperial War Museum, and thus a valuable archive will be available to all. Mr Wills' address is: Mr H. H. Wills, 5 Washern Close, Wilton, Salisbury, Wilts SP2 0LX.

Now you may think that with all this excellent work being put in by Mr Wills there is no future in becoming interested in pillboxes. But the opposite is the truth, for the local pillbox provides a superb focal point for military archaeology groups to congregate and also acts as a good group or individual project to get the 'feel' of the art, especially if it is a first attempt. Nearly every locality of the British Isles has a pillbox remaining somewhere not too far away. If access is at all possible (and where private land is involved, obtain permission for access first) use the pillbox as the subject for a 'trial run'. Visit the site and, after noting the information for Mr Wills, try to work out why the pillbox was emplaced there in the first place. That alone will take some working out as many were placed in very odd locations. Then try to work out if the pillbox was sited by itself or as part of a local defence system. They were frequently positioned in groups of three or more to provide mutual defending fire. Very often this exercise will reveal the siting or existence of other pillboxes in the locality—I once tried this and found an almost untouched example hidden beneath brambles about half a mile away. In many cases further investigation will reveal concrete obstacles nearby, often hidden under grass or undergrowth.

Once you have started this investigation you should be well on the way to yet more searching. Try to discover which units manned the position when it was first erected. This will often involve the local Home Guard and a few questions in the right places will lead to finding someone who actually manned the pillbox. That should lead to the discovery of the weapons involved, the numbers on site, the rotas used and before you know it such historical data will lead to yet more facets of life in the United Kingdom between 1940 and 1945. In my experience out come the photographs, the memories and very often the odd souvenirs. Only the week before writing this I discovered that I had missed the chance of obtaining a 12-bore shotgun cartridge specially loaded and marked by the War Office for Home Guard use (they had special large-shot loadings). I missed that one but I have obtained several invaluable Home Guard manuals from my local contacts and the same thing can usually be done by anyone who takes the trouble to use such a relic as the local pillbox as the starting point for research.

But the task should not end there. Many people still regard pillboxes as eyesores and it must be admitted that in many cases their opinion is justified. Time does not act kindly to brickwork or concrete and all too often their interiors or environs are used as dumping grounds for all manner of rubbish and debris. Thus many are still demolished every year even though some of them would serve as valuable monuments in their own right. But today the military archaeologist has one valuable ally on his side and that is the cost of such an operation. The demolition often involves more cost than removal is worth and it should not be too difficult to persuade some local authorities that preservation is easier than destruction. All that this usually involves is a simple clearing operation and the sealing of entrances and embrasures. In many cases this could be done by a local group of enthusiasts—the result may not look very pretty but at least a valuable relic will have been preserved for future generations who will probably take more interest in such a relic of the past (what about the Napoleonic Martello Towers?).

To ensure the survival of many pillboxes a local preservation order may be necessary. To obtain such an order you will have to approach your local authorities and enquire as to the proper channels to be used—they vary from place to place. But in some places you may find that preservation has already been carried out for you, albeit unwittingly. In many cases pillboxes have been used for building foundations, while others have been converted into outhouses or garden sheds. One farmer I know near me has had one in use as a pig-sty for many years. Near the coasts many pillboxes have been incorporated into seaside cottages or have been enlarged into garages or even kiosks.

Thus for the military archaeologist the humble pillbox can provide a wealth of interest. Whether as an object of interest in its own right, as part of a local defence network or as an object worthy of preservation, it can provide the military archaeology novice with a great deal of scope.

ST 898603 RMSW. A gun shelter built as part of the GHQ Line.

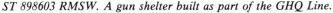

Chapter 6

Digging for the past

To most people the phrase 'military archaeology' will suggest a branch of conventional archaeology, which immediately conjures up the image of someone digging a hole in the ground. As this book has attempted to show, military archaeology means much more than this but in some instances a group or a couple of individuals will want to dig over a site to discover evidence or relics of military activity from some time in the past. This section cannot possibly cover every aspect of such excavations but hopefully it will outline some of the main points to be carried out or avoided.

One of the first points to be raised is why such digging is necessary at all. The answer is that very often it isn't, especially when a military site is marked by concrete structures pushing their way through undergrowth. But as mentioned elsewhere many military camps, depots and the like were only meant to be temporary structures and once the prefabricated buildings had been removed from a site when the military moved on or out, there was very little to show for their presence on the surface. In such cases the historian or archaeologist will want to know the exact location and extent of these sites and digging may be necessary. Another factor is that all too often the elements and natural erosion combine to hide a site in a remarkably short space of time, especially near coasts where some of the most interesting sites were located. Coastlines are notoriously mobile in some areas and many coast batteries and observation posts which were hurriedly constructed in both World Wars were built on shifting sub-strata or too close to the edges of eroding cliffs. One example of this was the coast battery at Hunstanton which had to be abandoned within a year of its construction owing to the cliffs eroding away nearby. The Channel Islands have several examples of bunkers collapsing into sand—some are still completely buried and await excavation.

The first step in any excavation is the necessary research and investigation into as many sources as possible regarding the accurate location of the site. This may be an obvious step to take but it is one which may save a great deal of time and effort and it also has an important safety aspect. Many defensive sites incorporated minefields and to this day some of those minefields still exist. Some have been forgotten and some are known but have not yet been cleared for any number of reasons. One reason may be sheer difficulty of access. A site may be approachable on foot but to get a lorry and heavy gear to the same place can be much more difficult. Another reason is the sheer number of land mines which were laid between 1940 and 1943— they ran into millions and to clear them will take years yet. So the survey exercise is an important one. The first people with whom to check are the landowners themselves. If the ground to be covered is in private hands this is a step which must be taken anyway. If the ground is owned by a local authority or is common land the local council or body should have the plans of any danger areas in their domain. The Royal Engineers are the military body responsible for mine clearance and they

Left *The mortar fuze that the author found on his first metal detector sweep. It had to be exploded the very next day.* **Right** *This 18 pr shell was discovered during an excursion to the Great War battlefields but it is typical of the lethal hardware that can still be found almost anywhere the services have been stationed (Ken Musgrave).*

maintain bomb and mine clearance units but the bulk of the area clearing work is done by a few small civilian teams, mainly composed of Ukranians who came to the United Kingdom during or just after the last war. They still travel around the British coastline gradually clearing the mines by the time-honoured process of mine-detector and hand removal.

If the safety aspect is resolved and the exact location of a site is known, clearing can then commence. This is the stage which usually separates the really dedicated from the mildly enthusiastic for it will often entail a great deal of sheer hard work and drudgery. Even clearing a small site for investigation frequently means shifting areas of undergrowth which are all too often littered with the debris and rubbish of years. At the same time as clearing starts it is often a good idea to give the area a sweep with a metal detector.

Metal detectors are an area of controversy at present. Properly used they can be invaluable aids to archaeology but of late they have often proved the opposite. It is now not uncommon for a metal detector operator to come across a hoard of coins or treasure and as a result sales of the detector have soared. Many have been sold to people who intend to use them for no other purpose than pure treasure seeking, which in itself is no bad thing but in many areas their digging and disturbing of valuable archaeological sites has done untold damage. Responsible and sensible use of metal detectors will prevent recriminations and trouble with responsible bodies but all too often the mere sight of a detector will raise the wrath of dedicated archaeologists.

Perhaps a word on metal detectors will not go amiss. Lately they have been sold by the thousand and a glance through the pages of *Exchange and Mart* or one of the several magazines devoted to the activity will give an idea of the models and the prices on the market. Price will be an important factor for many and they start at around £20-£25. Above that the sky seems the limit with higher prices going with greater sensitivity and operating depth. There are two main types. One operates on the old mine-detector principle in which a current is passed through a wire coil or coils. The coil sets up a small electrical field in which any metal object in the vicinity will create a disturbance, indicated on the instrument by a meter needle movement or an aural signal in headphones or on a loudspeaker. The other type utilises a magnetic principle and is known as the Proton Magnetometer—it detects anomalies in the Earth's magnetic field caused by metal objects and operates on the same principle as that used by aircraft searching for submarines in the ocean. For the

Left *Not only shells and debris are still being uncovered in France. This 21 cm howitzer barrel was discovered not so long ago near Sanctuary Wood (Ken Musgrave).* **Right** *Typical metal detector in use (C Scope Metal Detectors (UK) Ltd).*

operator the main difference is that a licence is needed for the coil type—your local Post Office will advise you of the procedure. Don't be put off by the need for a licence—it costs but £1.20 and it will last for five years.

The function of a metal detector when site clearing is to avoid disturbing any relic which might lie hidden just under the surface or in undergrowth. Many people's idea of site clearing entails swinging a great big shovel or spade with great gusto and as a result any small items could be damaged. Another reason is once again safety. Servicemen are notoriously careless with explosive hardware and often tend to disregard the odd shell or round that goes astray. In wartime there are a lot more important things to worry about than clearing up after an exercise so all too often there are sites which are littered with still-lethal debris. I have had a sample of this myself. Not so long ago I was taken to the site of a 1939-1945 small arms range on the South Downs, not far from my home. My guide took me to a series of natural re-entrants in the sides of the Downs where he has long been using a metal detector to find old and spent cartridge cases and even such things as cap badges. I had a go myself and on my very first sweep detected a signal which came from a very suspicious-looking mortar bomb fuze. It was re-buried where it lay and the next day the local Army Bomb Disposal Team arrived, took one look at it and blew it up on the spot! Just my luck.

When the surface is cleared the excavations proper can proceed. If you are searching for something as precise as a bunker or magazine entrance you should have a pretty good idea of where to start digging. But if you are simply carrying out an exploratory excavation to discover exactly what lies under a stretch of ground a bit more care in approach is needed. One of the worst things you can do is just pile in with everyone shovelling away frantically—the task has to be approached rather more carefully than that. There are several methods of carrying out methodical excavation but one of the most commonly used is the trench method. This entails digging a narrow trench in a prescribed straight line right across the area to be covered. This trench need not be very wide and as we are likely to be investigating only the last 50-60 years it need not be very deep—it is unlikely to go down more than 18 inches/450 mm. Mark out the line to be followed by string and pegs and keep the number of diggers to a minimum. Anyone left standing around can be detailed to examine the spoil for anything that might turn up—again a metal detector can come in handy but gentle probing with a trowel is the usual method.

If the first trench shows any signs of anything interesting the next step is to dig another narrow trench across it at right angles with the intersection at the most promising part of the first trench. When this second trench is completed there is very often little else to do unless the area is rich in finds such as small objects or several layers of foundations. By using this criss-cross system the outline of any concrete foundations can be acurately measured or assessed and the ground itself is not disturbed any more than necessary. Of course there are other methods but the narrow exploratory trench features in most of them and very rarely are our type of military archaeologists likely to have to carry out the detailed area investigations of those who excavate the distant past. If that is felt necessary the best I can do is suggest that your local museum will be far better equipped to advise you than I am as it is very much a specialist subject. All I suggest the average person should attempt is the simple exploratory dig that I have outlined, and no more.

But I must return once more to the peevish subject of safety as land mines are not the only items likely to be discovered in our islands. The Home Guard was reduced to some fairly desperate measures in its attempts to arm itself against potential invaders during the grim days of 1940 and 1941. Anti-tank defence was a priority but there were few weapons available in those days and the number of extemporised weapons was great as a result. Grenades were among the many weapons improvised and some of them were likely to be as dangerous to the thrower as the target. Among this total were the 'Sticky Bombs' and the 'Phosphorous Bombs'. The Sticky Bomb

The 'Iron Harvest' still found every year under the French Great War battlefields. This selection is the result of ploughing over just one farm (Ken Musgrave).

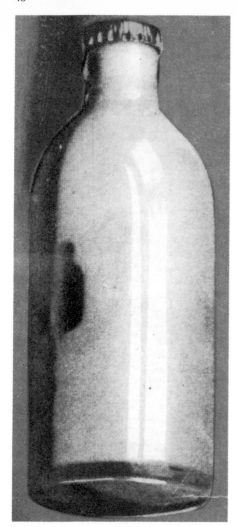

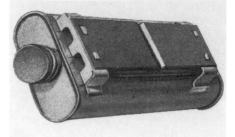

These pictures show items that may still be discovered but should be approached with great care. The Police should be informed when anything resembling these is discovered. **Left** *This innocuous-looking milk bottle is really filled with phosphorous suspended in a petrol solution. The results of breaking one can be imagined.* **Top** *The No 75 Hawkins grenade was intended for use not only as an anti-tank weapon but also as a mine. As a result they may still be dug up.* **Below** *The No 74 ST sticky bomb. Originally intended for anti-tank use, many were buried after 1945 as they proved too unsafe to move far.*

was shaped like a toffee apple with the head (the apple) coated with a gooey sticky substance which was supposed to make it adhere to the target tank. The Phosphorous Bomb was a milk bottle, or something similar, filled with phosphorous suspended in a petrol solution. Both types proved to be rather unsafe in use and thankfully very few were ever used in anger but when the time came for them to be withdrawn from service they proved, not surprisingly, to be rather unstable. Consequently some quite large caches were buried in various out-of-the-way spots to be dealt with at a later date. Needless to say that date very rarely arrived and many of these caches were forgotten. From time to time they are found, sometimes by accident and sometimes tragically, but the military archaeologist is more likely than most to discover them as he will be raking around where they were left. If anything suspicious does emerge under the spade or trowel the first thing to remember is *don't touch it* and make sure no-one else does. If possible the object should be reburied and some form of marker placed to show exactly where it is—this will save time later. Then inform the police who will alert the local Bomb Disposal Squad.

Nearly every area of the country has a squad on stand-by all the year round but they are usually kept pretty busy and so may not be able to arrive immediately. If it is at all possible someone should be on hand as a guide when they arrive and in any case, a responsible person should be on guard to prevent the unwary from approaching.

The main thing to remember is: don't try any bomb disposal yourself. Every year people in France and Belgium (and elsewhere) try it and are either killed or maimed by the resultant explosions. Care, common sense and a sense of public responsibility will prevent injuries.

The remote risk of injury aside, digging up the recent military past can be a most rewarding occupation. Unfortunately the chances of its application are rather limited in our overcrowded community but the results can be most illuminating and interesting. If the research preliminaries are carried out thoroughly the chances of finding something worth the effort are high. A great personal sense of history can be felt when something like a cap badge or belt buckle is unearthed for the first time in years.

One excellent example of this form of excavation was carried out during 1977 by the Jersey Branch of the CIOS who were given permission by the States of Jersey to uncover the fire control and command bunker of *Batterie Lotheringen* at Noirmont Point. The work entailed a great deal of hard manual labour for the bunker had been deliberately sealed by the States themselves in 1945 or 1946 and to re-open it was no mean task. Once inside more cleaning work had to be carried out but eventually it was ready for inspection and much to the surprise of the CIOS members the public came to see the site in droves. To add to the attraction of the two-storey underground rooms the CIOS have now started a gradual programme of removing as much of the remaining equipment as possible from other bunkers which are still exposed to the ravages of the elements and public perusal. This equipment, which includes such things as ventilation trunking and filters, electrical switch-boards and the like, is gradually being re-installed in the appropriate rooms in the renovated bunker and in time they will approach something like their origin..l appearance. In the meantime the CIOS will have an excellent meeting place and a worthwhile project on hand.

Further afield, in France there is still much that lies buried, and not only buildings. Weapons of all types still lie under Belgian as well as French soil, most of them emanating from 1914-1918 but the last great conflict left its mark and every year weapons and vehicles are discovered. Perhaps the example which best comes to mind is the Churchill tank that was dragged to the surface from under the sea wall near Arromanches a few years ago. That was a rather extreme example but lorries still lie hidden among the sand dunes of Normandy and here and there relics of tanks and half-tracks can be discovered at the backs of French garages and breakers' yards. But for reasons outlined elsewhere military archaeology in France and Belgium is very much a specialised and hazardous undertaking and a topic in itself.

Chapter 7

Motor vehicles

Without a doubt one of the most important innovations in warfare during the last 70-odd years has been the introduction of the internal combustion engine. Since its tentative appearance during the first decade of this century it has done much to revolutionise not only warfare but the social and industrial state of much of the world's population. Here we are primarily concerned with the warfare aspect, wherein the petrol or diesel engine has become one of the paramount components of the military machine for almost every extant army. During World War 1 it powered the first military motorised supply columns and by 1939 the use of the internal combustion engine allied with the caterpillar track and armour had converted the tank into a viable instrument of attack rather than a lumbering pillbox used to support infantry, which was all the World War 1 tanks were able to aspire towards. By 1939 most European armies were rapidly converting to mechanised supply and fighting formations but even in 1945 the horse was still an important element. (In 1939 the only fully mechanised army in the field in Europe was the little BEF contingent.) By 1945 all the major combatants had come to rely on the motor lorry for the bulk of their logistic support but here and there, especially in the Axis armies, the horse and mule were still in service.

Ask any Allied soldier who served between 1939 and 1945 how he was transported into battle and he will almost invariably answer that he was carried by lorry at some stage or other. Ask any second-line or defence soldier how he was supplied with food and all the other necessaries and he will again reply that lorries were involved. A service career was the first introduction to the internal combustion engine for many men in 1914-1918 and the same process was repeated for many more between 1939 and 1945. Not surprisingly, therefore, the military transport vehicle or AFV often became associated with the war periods to a greater extent than would happen today. Old soldiers still look back with something approaching affection for the vehicles they drove, or in which they were carried. This affection was often carried over into 'Civvy Street' after both wars when large numbers of ex-military vehicles were dumped on to the war surplus markets of the world. Huge numbers of lorries, staff cars and AFVs (stripped of weapons) were bought for relatively small sums during the 1920s and the years just after 1945. Many went for scrap but others were converted for the day-to-day purposes of peacetime commerce. A few were carefully put aside as collector's pieces or sold to museums but the numbers involved were small.

Very few military vehicles from World War 1 now remain in private hands. Most of the survivors are in museums and even fewer are still capable of use on any road. But World War 2 is another story. Not only were vastly greater numbers of military vehicles produced and used between 1939 and 1945 than between 1914 and 1918 but a far greater proportion of those who saw military service were trained to look after and drive them. Thus when they became available for commercial use there were far

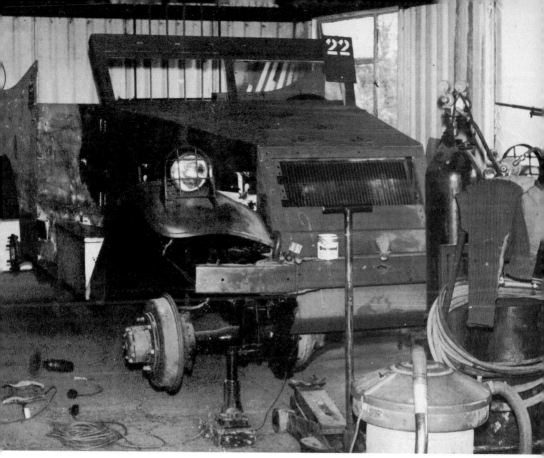

Above *A White Scout Car under renovation. This example was found in a quarry (Joe Lyndehurst).* **Below** *The finished product now on display at the Warnham War Museum.*

more people on hand to care for and use them. The result is that many ex-World War 2 vehicles are still with us today in running order and relics are being discovered all the time.

Whereas the first preservationists and collectors were usually ex-military people with a wish to preserve a piece of their past, the modern military vehicle collector and conservationist is a different bird. They are often people who wish to have a vehicle which is some form of tangible evidence of a major piece of history in which they were unable to participate. This is not the only reason why more and more people are being attracted to military vehicles for many now appreciate that such relics are gradually increasing in value, and that a good example of a wartime vehicle, whatever its provenance, is a worthwhile investment. A fair proportion of collectors simply like the idea of collecting miltiary vehicles or enjoy owning a single example just for the sake of it.

A visit to any miltiary vehicle rally or gathering will soon give any prospective vehicle enthusiast an idea of the spectrum of vehicle types which is available. Failing that a look through the columns of any copy of *Exchange and Mart* will give yet more information. The bulk of the vehicles which are collected or preserved are those that are small, easy to look after and store, and are readily available on the market. A smaller proportion of enthusiasts tend towards lorries and the like while at the top end of the interest scale are those who go in for the really large 6 × 4 lorries and such exotica as the amphibious DUKWs. Relatively few collectors manage to get hold of any AFVs and most of those held in private hands are the light reconnaissance vehicles such as Dingos and turretless Stuart tanks. But of all these different vehicle types the most popular is undoubtedly the Willys Jeep. This little 4 × 4 maid-of-all-work can be seen in large numbers at nearly all rallies, and as time goes by more and

This very battered Jeep was found in an overgrown orchard near Bognor Regis and despite its appearance it provided a wealth of spares to help restore less damaged vehicles (Joe Lyndehurst).

Awaiting their turn. An American GMC truck and a Canadian Chevrolet prior to restoration.

more are being avidly converted from everyday runabouts into prized and carefully restored museum pieces.

The attraction of the Jeep is understandable. It was used by nearly all the Allied armies for a multitude of purposes from runabouts to reconnaissance, signal and ambulance duties. To this day many are still in service all over the world (the Belgian Army still uses them for launching Entac anti-tank missiles). Thus the availability factor can be met relatively easily, and it should still continue in the years to come. A Jeep is small and thus need not take up too much storage or garage space. Repair and maintenance is fairly easy as a sizeable little industry has sprung up to supply spare parts and maintenance instructions. The cost of an unrestored and barely serviceable Jeep is not low—at the time of writing it is in the region of £500, but careful restoration will push the price tag up to around £2,000. For many individuals cost will be the limiting factor and consequently there has been an increasing trend over the last few years for groups of enthusiasts to band together to share costs.

But for all their ever-growing numbers, very few Willys Jeep are genuine wartime or early examples. Post-war and late production models can be altered and modified to resemble pre-1945 examples but the real enthusiast will spot them at a glance— the split windscreen is an easy identification feature on early models but there are many other points to note. Most collectors' Jeeps have been obtained via military surplus auctions but some are still available on the normal commercial second-hand market. The main trouble with the majority of ex-civil Jeeps is that they have usually been stripped of most military 'extras' such as panniers, brackets, stowage bins and such obvious military accoutrements as carbine holsters. To fully restore an ex-civil Jeep such items are essential and the real enthusiast will go to great lengths to obtain genuine parts. Such relatively small and innocuous parts as brackets and the like will thus fetch prices out of all proportion to their real value. Consequently scrap yards and derelict vehicles dumped in odd spots have attained great importance in the military vehicle restoration field.

The mention of scrap yards and derelict vehicles prompts me to mention that the military vehicle collection field is one which can involve a great deal of fieldwork. Numerous old lorries and vehicles have been dumped in the past in some very odd spots. Quarries and farmyards continue to provide happy hunting grounds for the vehicle enthusiast, for they can still throw up the unsuspected vehicle or spare part. Included with this section are examples of a derelict Jeep which provided invaluable

An excellent example of an early model of Willys Jeep still under restoration (Joe Lyndehurst).

parts for the restoration of another Jeep—itself found concealed in an orchard near Bognor—and a quarry was found to be the resting place of an almost complete White Scout Car not so long ago. Such fieldwork cannot be random and rumour and the inevitable enthusiast's grapevine become invaluable sidelines to the preservation and collecting pursuit. As time goes by such searchings will have to go further and further afield. Ireland and Northern France have both yielded some unusual collector's pieces but the Continent has now produced its own enthusiastic collectors who snap up anything they can. In many cases on the Continent they have to stand and watch some priceless relics getting literally ground and knocked to pieces. I myself know of a Panther tank chassis which is still in use to cart a crane around Normandy, and in Brittany a Somua half-track is rotting while a prolonged ownership suit is fought out in the courts.

To the layman the heaps of rusted metal and unrecogniseable metal parts that can make an enthusiast wild with excitement are just so much scrap. But to the preservationist they are the raw material. The process of restoring old military vehicles, whatever their size or type, is a lengthy and sometimes costly one, but it is not unduly difficult and specialist skills are rarely needed. Almost anyone who can manage to handle the usual standard metal- and wood-working tools should be able to undertake the work involved in restoring a military vehicle. In recent years the advent of the electric hand-drill and the range of accessories which can be obtained to fit it has made a large number of the more common tasks into relatively unskilled operations. The electric drill can be adapted for sanding, metal cutting, paint spraying, buffing and, of course, drilling, and even a small and low-priced drill can cover a range of jobs. Very few specialised tools are needed and if any specialist operations are encountered it is often cheaper in the long run to get them carried out commercially rather than invest in expensive plant.

Whatever the state of any new purchase or find, for really long-term preservation the vehicle will have to be stripped of all paint and other coverings right down to the bare metal. All rust and body rot will have to be removed drastically, and any part with even slight body-rot will have to be replaced with either new or replacement parts. Body rot on a vehicle is rusting which has become so advanced that the metal just flakes or rots away at a touch, and it usually becomes apparent on the underside and lower portions of the vehicle. In really advanced cases there is nothing for it but to rebuild the body with new metal panels—this may involve some extra cost but the end result will be worth the trouble. The chassis will have to be closely examined for damage or corrosion since it is the basis of any vehicle and no matter how well the visible metal and paint work is restored it will all be for naught if the chassis collapses. If a wooden tilt or other parts are involved it is usually best to replace them unless they are in very good condition—the same goes for leather seat coverings and the like, and canvas will usually have to be replaced as a matter of course.

Surprisingly enough, the engines, if they are still fitted, will usually be found to be in far better condition than the vehicle they are meant to power. Even today it is still possible to obtain spare parts and extras for many wartime engines and a little care and attention will make most seemingly derelict power units come to life again. The engine should, of course, be the charge of a skilled motor fitter but again maintenance manuals are still on the market for common models and appropriate paperwork can even be provided for some of the more obscure types. Again, these maintenance manuals are the currency for a small but thriving cottage industry as a small number of enthusiasts have discovered that searching for and providing

This Steyr staff car was once on show at the Beaulieu Motor Museum. It can now be seen at the Warnham War Museum.

manuals for others can be a worthwhile occupation in itself—and it can sometimes be made into a very lucrative pastime when really obscure documentation is involved.

By the time you have reached the stage of rebuilding panelwork and the like, the pictorial research stage should have been completed. Such research should not only have included a thorough study of the appropriate maintenance manuals, but a widespread search for as many pictorial references as possible. Most restoration buffs like to make their particular charge, or charges, as representative and accurate for their period as is humanly possible and the only way to do this is closely to examine photographs taken at the time when, and in the appropriate theatre of war where, the vehicle was in service. There are some well-illustrated books obtainable commercially on the topic of soft-skin vehicles in action, but not very many, so in many cases this pictorial research will have to be conducted through piles of old magazines or in the various photographic libraries. The largest of these picture libraries in the UK is that at the Imperial War Museum at Lambeth, but another can be perused at the Royal Corps of Transport Museum at Aldershot where a virtually untapped collection of pictures can be examined (and obtained). Other sources are scattered around but those two will meet most British collectors' needs. A period photograph can show all manner of details which can enhance any restoration project, ranging from tool and spares stowage to slight differences in door fittings, spare wheel stowage and bodywork. But for real authenticity, photographic sources *must* be studied for colouring and markings.

The finish can make or mar any vehicle. If a vehicle has been painted in the wrong paint shade or with the wrong markings in the wrong places it will almost always be glaringly obvious and detract from the appeal of an otherwise carefully carried-out piece of restoration. Fortunately most British and American vehicles of World War 2 used only a few basic colour schemes so this should be no problem. However, I have seen some vehicles which have been sprayed gloss instead of matt and for some people the shade known as 'sand' seems to cover everything from off-white to a lurid canary yellow. The only way to ensure that your efforts are correct is to indulge once

Although it will be some time before it will get the full restoration treatment, this DUKW has been stripped and primed with a good metal primer to try and keep off the worst ravages of the elements until space can be found for the full treatment.

Carrier, Universal, T16. Very popular at rallies but unfortunately often in demand for towing bogged-down vehicles from the mud attendant on so many such occasions.

more in research, and especially research into the correct size and placing of markings. Vehicle markings cover a fairly wide spectrum from the small tyre pressure labels carried on the wings to divisional and unit insignia. The latter is a wide field indeed and once more pictorial evidence should be closely examined for type and placings. Despite a wealth of evidence to the contrary, not every military truck and Jeep carried divisional or unit badges. Almost every formation had a pool of vehicles which were loaned out to lower units for specific tasks and these rarely carried any unit markings other than the standard identification signs (in North-West Europe from 1944 to 1945 this was the well-known five-pointed white star) and such mundane items as bridge-crossing classification and loading restrictions which were common to all transport and fighting vehicles. There are a few books on the subject of vehicle markings on the market but they are often difficult to find so the only real way to ensure authenticity and accuracy is (once more) through reference to photographic evidence.

One point which has not been mentioned up till now is that some form of cover is necessary, not only for restoration and rebuilding but also for storage once the job is finished. In almost any climate, prolonged exposure to the elements will soon return a restored vehicle to the state where you started from in a very short time, and for spraying and much of the basic groundwork, cover is a 'must'. For small vehicles such as Jeeps the ordinary household garage is perfectly adequate but anything larger will need more roomy premises. In the country a barn or outhouse can usually be found but in towns and cities adequate space can be an expensive proposition. This cost factor alone is one which can severely restrict preservation projects and is one of the main reasons why military vehicle ownership is often a group activity or the preserve of the well-off.

Despite the money aspect the military vehicle scene is expanding. Every year more and more old trucks and Jeeps are rescued from all sorts of horrible fates and are lovingly restored to their former states. Once completed their owners are understandably reluctant to hide their efforts from public scrutiny and this has resulted in the number of military vehicle rallies increasing from year to year. Not so

Army DUKWs at one of their last public appearances before they left full-time service with the RCT during the early 1970s.

long ago there were only one or two rallies attended by the faithful, and they were rarely advertised widely. Today such rallies are not only common, they are big affairs which attract vehicles and spectators from all over the country. One of the largest rallies of the year used to be held at Winkfield, near Windsor, but now that has been eclipsed by several other occasions, even if it does still remain as one of the biggest. These rallies are usually big and entertaining affairs where the dedicated enthusiast and Joe Public can rub shoulders for both business and pleasure. The business side is provided by the large number of stands and stalls selling everything from spares to uniforms, while the public get their money's worth from fairs and such spectacles as Peter Grey's 'Hell on Wheels' team.

Some have turned their hobby into more lucrative pastimes. Dotted around the country are various small museums formed from the collections of some of the more enthusiastic and successful preservationists. Such a collection can be seen in Sussex at the Warnham War Museum, not far from Horsham. Formed and run by Joe Lyndehurst, this excellent collection of vehicles is housed in a custom-built structure which covers not only the vehicles but also a fine collection of uniforms and ephemera. A visit to Warnham can show exactly what can be achieved in the vehicle preservation field, for the exhibits can be closely examined for detail, and can also serve as a good standard of detail and finish to aim for. Not only has each item been carefully preserved and researched, but it has been restored as nearly as possible to its original state and detail. Such items as stowage of camouflage netting, personal equipment and loads have been painstakingly reproduced in an almost exact recreation of their original service states.

Joe Lyndehurst's collection is not the only museum-based one of its kind but it is one of the best. Others can rarely show the public their collections except at rallies, but they earn their keep in other ways. Tony Oliver has a superb collection of German vehicles but they provide funds by being hired out for films and television appearances—the BBC 'Colditz' series was one well-known example. But perhaps the biggest potential collection is that of the Imperial War Museum. Space at Lambeth prevents the display of more than a very few items in this 'national' collection and the bulk of it is held at Duxford in Cambridgeshire, but unfortunately it is not open to the public except on a few rare public days. Most of the time the collection is kept under wraps and under cover for there is still much work to do on most of it, and the bulk of the work is carried out by volunteer enthusiasts. The majority of the vehicles at Duxford have been held in storage for many years and are consequently not always in a very good state—much work still awaits the enthusiast's hand.

Up till now mention has been made of the vehicles of World War 2 but it should not be forgotten that that conflict ended over 30 years ago. Since 1945 whole generations and families of vehicles have entered and left military service and as such are worthy of preservation in their own right. Many collectors have already snapped up such items as Austin Champs and a few have obtained Humber APCs, commonly known as 'Pigs', when they have been offered on the military surplus markets. The vast American surplus parks in the United Kingdom and in Europe can still provide the chance to obtain military vehicles at relatively cheap prices but with such big markets there is a large commercial lobby and only the really determined should attempt to purchase single items. The main point to realise is that such chances to obtain an ex-military vehicle will become rarer as the years go by and now is the time to purchase such commonplace types as Land-Rovers (even though they are still in production early examples are now becoming collectors' items) and Bedford four-tonners. Although they might be common today such vehicles will soon become rare, and one day they will be eagerly sought after. As ever, today's run-of-the-mill is tomorrow's rarity.

A short chapter like this cannot really do anything but skate over the surface of what is undoubtedly a large and wide-ranging subject. Anyone who is considering, or is about to embark on, vehicle conservation should contact one of the many groups which have sprung up all over the country, formed to exchange information

The interior of the Warnham War Museum.

Top end of the market. An American half-track fitted with a jib and used for light recovery work by the British REME until the 1970s. When they were retired they were avidly sought-after by the preservationists who could afford them and today they are prized possessions and exhibits (Joe Lyndehurst).

and enable people with a common interest to meet and exchange their views. To date there is no single overall body which oversees the entire military vehicle preservation scene, but several useful addresses are given at the back of this book to which interested persons should write. From personal experience I have found that one of the most useful and helpful contacts anyone can make is with the very knowledgeable staff of the Warnham War Museum. Their postal address is: Warnham War Museum, Warnham, Nr Horsham, West Sussex.

If they can't help they will be able to put you in touch with someone who can. All over the country there are small groups of enthusiasts who specialise in one particular type or group of vehicles and who deal with that one topic alone. There are groups who specialise in American motor cycles, Daimler Scout Cars, and many other similar vehicle types. Somewhere there will be someone who will be only too willing to help you, guide you, and give you advice.

Chapter 8

Badges, insignia and uniforms

The origins of the military cap badge, or emblem along with its associated art of heraldry, is lost in the dim mists of times gone past. Mention of military emblems can be found in the Old Testament and since then military bands and armies have usually adopted some form of emblem or sign for identification purposes, or have had one imposed to generate a form or measure of group loyalties. In our measurable history such emblems became associated with family or national loyalties and from them came the military emblems which are now used for modern military identification in the form of the cap badge. The British Army is still rich in this link with history. Nearly every badge still in use has associations with the past. Family and county emblems still abound along with signs of heraldry which have been established for centuries. To this day animals, birds, weapons and mystic emblems continue to adorn uniforms and badges as they have done for centuries. The humble Leek, first used as a national symbol when Cadwallader beat the Saxons back in AD 640, is still in use as the badge of the Welsh Guards, and the Stafford Knot has been a badge of the Staffordshire regiments for centuries.

Not surprisingly the military cap badge has become a much-prized artefact in its own right and in many regiments it has replaced the colours as an everyday symbol of regimental pride. For collectors and historians it has become a very much sought-after item and today military badge collecting is a widespread and expanding interest. Two World Wars and a turbulent military and social history have made the 20th Century one rich in military emblems, not only in the British services but in the armies of many other nations as well. Regiments have come and gone, never to return, specialist formations have adopted their own peculiar heraldry only to disband, never to be reformed, and distant regiments have traversed the globe. All that is left of many fine formations is a metal symbol of their existence in the shape of a cap badge. Almost any military badge which comes into the collector's hands has a tale to tell, some of them full of military glory, many of them from the ancient past and some with poignant memories. Researching and reading of such tales is a most interesting and rewarding facet of modern history and the years since 1900 abound with such relics and metal reminders.

To the layman the military cap badge is just an ornate piece of metal or cloth—to the soldier it is a bit more complex than that. For a start there are many differing types. A simple division can be made between the versions worn by officers and those issued for other ranks. In the British Army the officers usually wear a more ornate and finely-made badge than the simple stampings issued to NCOs and privates. In the early years the use of gold and silver for officers' badges was not uncommon on dress uniforms, but after 1914 gilt was the more usual metal used. For the other ranks brass in the shape of 'gilding metal' or 'white metal' was the normal medium, usually stamped from a single sheet. Variations were numerous and in times of raw material shortages plastic or bakelite were used, while today the use of anodised

Being a Londoner I have always had some interest in the London Regiments, and their cap badges were usually fairly easy to find. Now nearly all the regiments shown here have passed away, and the collection shown would be difficult to replace. **Top row,** *left to right: London had only one Regular Infantry Regiment, the Royal Fusiliers (City of London Regiment) and it formed the parent regiment for the first four City of London Battalions; 7th (City of London) Battalion, The London Regiment (in being 1908-1922); 15th (County of London) Battalion, The London Regiment. Also known as the Prince of Wales' Own, or the Civil Service Rifles; The Rangers, The King's Royal Rifle Corps, originally the 12th County of London Regiment; 13th County of London Regiment (Princess Louise's Kensington Regiment).* **Middle Row,** *left to right: 19th (County of London) Battalion, The London Regiment (St Pancras); 5th City of London Regiment (London Rifle Brigade); 14th (County of London) Battalion, The London Regiment (London Scottish); 25th (County of London) Cyclist Battalion, The London Regiment (extant 1908-1922); Royal Engineers (Volunteers). Not strictly an exclusive London formation but typical of the many formations 'found' by Londoners.* **Bottom row,** *left to right: 10th County of London Regiment (Hackney); Inns of Court Regiment; Shoulder badge of 8th (City of London) Battalion, The London Regiment; 17th County of London Regiment—also known as Tower Hamlets Rifles; 23rd (County of London) Battalion, The London Regiment.*

plastic or alloys is commonplace. Associated with the badges were hackles, colour facings and variations in uniform colours or styles, all of them fervently guarded from outside interventions of military fashion or organisation. The British Army is not alone in this retention of links with the past. Abroad nearly every army contains formations which jealously retain links with their past, and the end result is a happy hunting ground for the collector, as well as a repository of historical wealth for the student.

Up until 1914 the British Army was formed from a relatively small number of regular Line regiments along with numerous county and city Territorial and Yeomanry regiments. The events of 1914 and after prompted an enormous expansion in the number of men under arms and with this expansion came an increase in the numbers of regimental battalions. Men flocked to join up, only to be turned away as the Army could not absorb them, and in the meantime there emerged one of the most interesting badge forms of the Great War. Volunteers were issued with small lapel badges to show that they had offered their services to the Crown and in time these badges were also issued to war industry workers to show they were also 'doing their bit'. Until recently the collecting of such badges has been a relatively low-key occupation, but of late they have become much sought-after pieces, and I consider myself lucky that I picked up the few I now have when I had the chance.

After 1914, once a volunteer had joined up he was often part of what were known as the 'Pals Battalions'. These formations proved to be one of the more poignant military mistakes of the Great War, for their name gives an indication of their origins. Men were urged and encouraged to join up with their 'pals', whether from work, a sports association or from a common place of residence. The idea was to generate unit pride from a common association, and initially the result was the formation of the finest volunteer army the world has ever seen. Many of these 'Pals Battalions' were issued with their own badges, even though they were usually affiliated to an existing regiment or corps, and they proudly carried their new emblems over to France. The sad results came from the peculiar nature of the

Ideally it would be nice to have the complete belts rather than just these two buckles. The top buckle is of the Royal Marines Light Infantry, while the bottom one has been separated to show the matching numbers, ie, a '3', just visible on each section. The buckle is an example that once belonged to an officer from the Army Vehicle Reserve prior to 1914.

Western Front fighting. Attacks 'over the top' were usually made in battalion strength across the lethal wastes of 'No-mans Land' and as a result those 'Pals Battalions' were decimated, often in minutes. The Somme battles of 1916 saw the last of them, and the few survivors were absorbed by other battalions. Back home, each district of the towns and cities and each country area took its turn to receive squads of telegraph boys bearing tidings of the casualty figures and by the end of 1916 there were few parts of the nation that had not been plunged into collective mourning. Even the little Channel Island of Guernsey did not escape. In 1914 the island militia volunteered for regular service and became the Royal Guernsey Light Infantry. They went over the top on the first day of the Somme Offensive and even today the lists of names on the war memorial in St Peter Port are an awful reminder of a lost generation which a small island could never replace. Today the 'Pals' have few memorials, and their badges have become rarities.

The Great War had many other odd formations which were assembled for the duration only. The Machine Gun Corps did not survive long after 1918 and the Naval Battalions were expedients only. World War 2 produced another crop of oddities such as the Reconnaissance Corps which lasted only from 1943 to 1946, but the example of the 'Pals' was not repeated. Instead the Home Guard created its own local insignia and in many cases adopted its own form of heraldry which has since

Taking photographs in showcases in museums can be difficult as odd reflections intrude and very often flash is impossible due to flash 'bounce' back into the lens. The best way is to select a position with the minimum of reflections and use both a time exposure and a tripod. This little group is in the Warnham War Museum and shows (bottom) a Royal Flying Corps Captain's working uniform. Right behind it is the tunic and bandolier belonging to a gunner of the Royal Horse Artillery in the Great War. Next to it the leather belt shows that the original owner belonged to the local Home Guard.

As mentioned in the text American uniforms are very popular with many collectors who like to appear as authentic as possible. Not one of the persons in this picture is a genuine American soldier—they are all British civilians (Joe Lyndehurst).

become a specialist collector's delight. The existence of many Allied armies in the United Kingdom also produced a large amount of foreign insignia and badges for future generations to seek after. The years since 1945 have seen numerous upheavals in the British Army structure as successive defence rearrangements have amalgamated regiments and corps only to place them into limbo under yet more reorganisations. Many old regiments have now gone for ever and in their place a drastic reshuffle of formations has resulted in new badges and new corps. Consequently the old badges are now virtually unobtainable through the channels which were current when I started my little collection many years ago. Then badges could be obtained for pennies or for nothing if you asked the right people.

The same cannot be said today. At the time of writing the collecting of military badges, including the various cloth badges and the odd facings and variations, has become a minor cottage industry. Prices have risen year by year until now one has to fork out at least £1 for the least distinguished and most common of badges. 'Pals' badges can fetch around £30 and some rarities sell for much more. A glance at most seller's catalogues or lists will show that most examples are in the £1 to £5 price range, and most collar badges (or collar dogs) will cost about the same—but make sure they are matched, ie, the symbols should face inwards where appropriate. Thus assembling a new collection from scratch *can* entail a considerable outlay, but I still seem to be able to pick up the odd item here and there relatively cheaply. Searching for badges in odd junk shops or jumble sales can still produce the odd 'find', but of

During both World Wars numerous British Commonwealth and Empire units have come to the United Kingdom and left their cap badges behind them. The selection above is but a tiny sample. **Top row,** *left to right: 8th Battalion, Winnipeg Light Infantry; West Nova Scotia Regiment; 1st South African Infantry; Royal Canadian Army Pay Corps; 35th Sikhs.* **Middle row,** *left to right: Top, Royal Deccan Horse; Bottom, Canadian Regiment; Royal Natal Carabiners; Toronto Scottish; Royal Canadian Ordnance Corps; Top, Cyprus Regiment; Bottom, Indian Engineers collar badge.* **Bottom row,** *left to right: 7th Australian Light Horse; St John Fusiliers, Newfoundland; 1st Canadian Regiment shoulder badge.*

late I have begun to notice that only cloth badges are obtainable from such sources. These cloth badges are not usually regimental badges but are those issued for tradesman and specialist soldiers such as farriers, snipers and signallers, to quote but a few examples.

The other form of cloth badge is the divisional sign worn on the upper arm or the regimental title worn at the top of the sleeve. Divisional signs are as varied as regimental badges and for many collectors they form an interest of their own. These sleeve badges were as common in overseas armies as they were for the British, and in many cases the same insignia was often used on vehicles as well. Most divisional insignia consisted of geometric shapes and signs only (especially in the German services) but others were more complex. Perhaps the best source of information on the subject can be found in *Formation Badges of World War 2*, by Howard Cole (Arms and Armour Press), but other works on the subject are available. The Cole book deals with British and Commonwealth insignia only, but there are books in the Profile series which cover German and American usage. While discussing books, one of my constant references for British badges has been *Regimental Badges*, by Major J. Edwards (published now by Charles Knight), but again there are many other works available.

The sudden and rapid expansion in badge collecting over the last few years has led to some rather dubious practices being inflicted on the unwary buyer. One such practice is the use of old stamping dies to produce 'restrikes' which are sold as genuine articles. Some would argue that the use of the old dies, many of them the same dies which were used for the original production runs, does not constitute sharp practice, but the discriminating collector will want badges that have 'seen service' and not commercial restrikes, even if they can be used to fill temporary gaps in a collection. The trouble now is that so many restrikes have been made and sold that they have become difficult to detect. When buying a metal cap badge look for signs of wear that show the badge has been cleaned in the past and beware of brass badges with a semi-gloss sheen which shows they have never seen Brasso. A usual certificate of authenticity on some older badges is the soldier's number, or 'last three', stamped on the fixing prong, but this is not all that common and its absence does not mean it is a restrike.

One facet of badge collecting which is awash with reproductions and fakes is the very popular field of World War 2 German badges and insignia. Ever since 1945 the various German service badges and Nazi gew-gaws have been eagerly sought-after and demand has constantly outstripped supply. The supply has been met by an ever-growing stream of fakes which has become progressively more difficult to detect, and one expert has told me that nearly three-quarters of the items shown to him recently have been fakes. To the uninitiated the differences between the real thing and the fake can be so difficult to spot that they will not worry, but the discriminating collector will not want to pay out considerable sums of money for a reproduction, no matter how good it is. So the only motto to adopt when buying German badges, as with edged weapons, is 'let the buyer beware'.

The same goes for another facet of collecting which is not too far from badges and insignia, namely the collecting of steel helmets. Both World Wars have produced a great variety of styles and shapes of helmet but to this day the most popular collector's item still remains the German *Stahlhelm*. Once again commercial interests have tried to meet the demand for these relics by commercial reproductions but very often these fakes are relatively easy to spot—usually their condition is too good for their age.

If collectors go to the length of collecting steel helmets it is but a short step to the

The Services still retain quite large stocks of old uniforms for display purposes. These troopers are from the Royal Tank Regiment and are in the uniform of the Great War cavalry.

Tattoos and band concerts are good places to see how uniforms used to look before fatigues and camouflage colours became the norm, as illustrated by this picture of the King's Troop, Royal Horse Artillery taken at the Aldershot Army Display.

acquisition of complete uniforms. Uniforms from the earliest years of the century onwards are still obtainable because many old soldiers took them home with them for possible reserve service once their regular terms had expired, and the Territorials kept their uniforms at home anyway. Consequently many still turn up on the market, very often in excellent condition. But even now uniform collecting is not a very popular pastime for several reasons. Storing an old uniform is no easy task and considerable trouble and time is needed to prevent the ravages of the clock and the House Moth. Even so there are many uniform collectors who take great pride in their chosen subject and devote considerable time and effort to maintaining and displaying the complete uniforms of bygone regiments and corps.

Just as important as the uniform itself are the correct badges and insignia, and all the various other accoutrements such as belts and headgear. For various reasons, not the least of which is availability and a relatively small outlay of cash, American uniforms are a well-established commodity at motor vehicle rallies and close runners-up in popularity are British World War 2 battledress uniforms or fatigues. In both cases one of the main attractions is the extra degree of authenticity and accuracy which their wearers can bestow on their carefully restored vehicles, but it is obvious to many observers that in some cases the uniform is worn just for the fun of it, and for the opportunity of sublimating everyday life in an advanced form of fantasy, just for a short while.

Whatever form of collecting you might undertake, be it badges, insignia or uniforms, you will find it a most rewarding one. Once you start to amass badges or insignia you will soon find that collecting them produces its own particular form of 'bug', and it is a form which bites rather deeply. I obtained my first badges when I was about six years old and ever since then part of me has been constantly on the look-out for the merest hint of a cap badge which is remotely obtainable. My personal collection is still a modest one compared with many, but it is a constant source of interest and pleasure and I hope I will never be parted from it.

A short note on medals

Mention of badges and insignia to a collector will often bring up the subject of medals. I have deliberately not gone into the subject for the simple reason that it has become an area where costs have risen so sharply and dramatically that the average collector or enthusiast cannot possibly get a look-in. Despite the rather distasteful aspect of the topic, the sale of gallantry awards and campaign medals has now become big business as even a quick glance at the advertisements placed in the national Press and magazines will soon show. Before long, dealers will have scooped the market and then prices will rise even more, so if you have any good or unusual medals, and especially if they are in unusual groupings or combinations, all I can say is hang on to them, or better still, pass them on to their appropriate regimental institute or museum where they will get the respect they deserve.

In the meantime I'm hanging on to my Royal Observer Corps Long Service medal!

*This little grouping consists of lapel badges worn by those who attempted to offer their services to the Army or Navy in 1914 but were turned down, either because they were in important jobs already, or because they could not be taken on at the time. The Veterans Reserves were made up of ex-soldiers who were technically too old for further service but in time they too were taken on full-time to take over home duties and free younger men for service overseas. These badges were originally worn to deter the more strident 'white feather' merchants who were so much a feature of the Home Front after 1914. **Top row,** left to right: On War Service, 1915 (the LGOC denotes London General Omnibus Company); On War Service, 1915 (issued to armaments workers); On War Service, 1914 (issued to clerical workers in the Civil Service). The Veteran Reserve badges are explained above but the long oval badge in the bottom row is of the Athletes' Volunteer Force, 1914. This was one of the earliest 'Pals' units and was issued prior to the volunteers getting their uniforms.*

Chapter 9

The voices of war

As mentioned in the introduction to this book, one of the most important projects the military archaeologist can undertake is the recording of the memories of those who were eye witnesses during the many major and minor conflicts which have taken place during the 20th Century. There are two main methods of doing this: one is by interviewing the eye witness and writing down, either in shorthand or longhand, their answers to questions or promptings; and the other is by using a tape recorder actually to record their voices as they recall their experiences. Both have their place for the historian but of the two I would suggest the tape recorder has several advantages. One is that transcribing speech on to paper is a lengthy process and a great deal can be missed by subsequent editing or the wrong interpretation of written passages which are often at variance with their original meanings. Another drawback is that the final transcriptions are frequently difficult to read, and all too often a well-told story makes only a poor manuscript.

Tape recorders can overcome the disadvantages of transcribing spoken prose and they have many positive advantages. For a start, the tape itself, once recorded, is an end product and very often little or no editing is necessary. If the recording itself is carried out properly the voice of the interviewee can very often carry a sense of occasion and action that the written word so often lacks (unless of course the person is highly literate, and there are few of us that have that gift). A big advantage for many will be that the actual recording of a tape entails relatively little work while transcribing a conversation can be an irksome chore.

Having listed a few advantages that the use of tape recorders have over other recording methods, I must mention that these advantages only apply if our old friends, planning and a clear objective, are applied. Just because the act of setting up a small microphone and a tape deck is relatively easily done it does not follow that a useful recording will result automatically. Successful and useful recordings will only be achieved by advance planning and preparation—without these two stages recordings will all too often become mere taped ramblings and unconnected snatches of memories that are of little use to anyone in the future.

The selection of suitable recording equipment is no longer a major problem these days as the electronic revolution continues to place an ever-growing array of goodies within the price ranges of more and more of the population. Not so long ago tape recorders were bulky and expensive gadgets but now everyone is familiar with the small cassette recorder and the models on the market grow gradually smaller and smaller in size as they become progressively easier to use. There are some very highly specialised speech recorders on the market but they are often expensive and not very portable while at the other extreme are the small pocket recorders or 'voice notebooks' that are not really intended for long-term recordings at all. I would suggest that for most of the work the average military archaeologist is likely to carry out the common-or-garden cassette recorder is all that is necessary. As long as the recorder has a decent hand or table microphone and can accommodate a standard cassette all should be well. The price to be paid will depend on each individual's (or group's) finances, but bear in mind that some of the very cheapest equipment is not meant to be durable. Again, when selecting the tapes themselves I would suggest that, while it is often not necessary to buy the best quality tapes obtainable, it is best to avoid the very cheapest.

Having obtained, or organised, the recording equipment, the really hard work comes with selecting the people to be recorded. I have suggested in the introduction that as many people as possible should be recorded for posterity and especially those who lived through World War 1. This should be the main priority but let us not forget that apart from those who went through the dreadful years from 1939 to 1945 there have been many other major and minor conflagrations in our violent century. Between the wars there were all the various actions in Mesopotamia and the continuing skirmishing on the North-West Frontier of India. Since 1945 there has been Malaya, Korea, Cyprus, Aden, Borneo and many other such campaigns and wars. These too deserve the recording treatment before everything is forgotten or gets jumbled with other memories. So the selection band is a wide one, so wide in fact that selection is not easy.

One of the first steps in selection is to discover whether or not the person wants to be recorded and, if they do, whether they have anything worth recording. From my own experience this is best done by personal contact, although some enterprising historians have advertised in local and national newspapers or magazines for specific periods and have thereby obtained some fascinating material. But I have found that in any social circle such as the local pub or club there is almost always someone with something worth telling. I used to frequent one pub, some years ago, with an old boy who had been through most of the Great War with a horse artillery unit, and the tales he used to tell over a pint were well worth listening to, even if only half of what he said was what actually happened. (It was from him that I learned that the practice of 'fragging' unpopular NCOs or officers with grenades, which was so publicised during the Vietnam War, was a not uncommon practice between 1914 and 1918.) In my present local I have spoken to a man who landed on the Normandy beaches before D-Day to obtain sand samples, to another who was involved in the forcible repatriation of Russian prisoners-of-war to Russia after 1945, and to another who spent most of his service life billeted-out in his own home. All of them would make fascinating and useful recording subjects but in at least one case I have run into the problem that they do not wish to be recorded.

This problem is a not uncommon phenomenon in the recording field and it has several origins. One is pure diffidence in that some people feel they have nothing to hand on to posterity, and in many cases this will be true. But in other cases the opposite is the case and considerable powers of persuasion may have to be brought into play to make them alter their attitude. Another cause is a much more painful and understandable one as some people went through such harrowing and horrific experiences that they have spent much time since trying to erase their memories—to recall them is too awful to bear. Obviously even the keenest historian will not try to pry into such cases, and if they did they would probably not like what they heard. Other people might have real or imagined speech problems which prevent them speaking into a microphone, and so the list continues.

But once a selection has been made and a readiness to participate has been expressed, it is still only the preliminaries to the actual recording. It is no use just plonking down a recorder and starting the chat, for to get the maximum usefulness from the exercise there is still much to do. Most of it will consist of general conversation, unrecorded on tape but with general notes being made on a notepad of the more interesting points which should be included in the final recording. These conversations can be fascinating and full of interest and very often one will be overwhelmed with a mass of information, much of it very detailed. When I first got involved in this field I was amazed at the seemingly trivial details which emerged from such conversations, often from people who I knew had difficulty in remembering where they were only a few days previously. Once I had mentioned this point to a few people I discovered that such memory detail is not uncommon for the simple reason that for all too many the war period and its attendant pressures and stresses were the only things worth remembering which had ever happened to them—the day-to-day civilian experiences were soon submerged in a mass of routine.

Other points to note at this stage are anything that does not ring quite true or is at odds with what is known. This does not necessarily mean deliberate embellishment (although it must be constantly watched for) but is all too frequently the result of time mixing up occasions and facts. In my own experience I have encountered an old soldier who was convinced that the American 75 mm Pack Howitzer was the same thing as the British 3.7-inch Pack Howitzer. Even after only a short passage of time such lapses are understandable, but corrections must be made tactfully and with care.

From the conversations a script should emerge which should contain and list in order the points to be covered in the recording. This *must* be shown to and agreed with the person to be recorded and the need to adhere to its points should be tactfully stressed. The script need not be a word-for-word manuscript—often a list of main headings is all that is necessary, along with questions and prompting points. Ideally the final recording should contain the main 'meat' of the preceeding conversations but this should not mean that all the details or trivia should be omitted—they can frequently convey a sense of period and atmosphere far better than bare facts.

With all these preliminaries made and agreed to the actual recording itself can commence. The best place to make the recording is usually the home of the person being interviewed for it is there that they will most feel at ease, but first check the premises for any factors such as noise or disturbances which will detract from the quality of the final recording. Once settled a few test recordings and play-backs will not only check-out the equipment but will put everyone into a more relaxed state—it is surprising how the mere sight of a microphone will cause many people to change the pitch of their voice or manner of speech, but usually all will be back to normal after a few minutes.

Ideally each recording should commence with the recorder (the operator) giving a brief introduction to the person to be recorded and a short outline of the material to be covered. If you feel like it the recording date should be included as well. With the introduction out of the way the recording proper can begin. The recorder should keep his questioning and prompting to a minimum—this sounds obvious but I have heard some efforts in which the interviewer hogged most of the recording time with his own opinions and comments. If the preparations have been carried out correctly and thoroughly all should go well. If it hasn't the session will deteriorate into an ill-organised and rambling chat with little content and only limited interest.

Opinions will vary as to how long each recording should last. Some seem to go on for ever and when the content is good this is no problem. My own opinion is that 30 minutes is enough for each session—more can be organised as and when necessary.

Once completed the tape should be played back to the person recorded. If all is as it should be and no corrections or amendments need to be made the tape cassette should be clearly labelled with the subject matter, date of recording and time of running. It should then be stored in a secure place and a summary of its contents placed into some form of central filing system, for if you carry out the recording task properly you will very soon amass a pile of cassettes and some form of filing system will be needed.

The subject then arises as to the final resting place of all this taped history. Unless such work is spread to reach everyone who might need it, it is useless. One problem is that, as yet, such recorded material is not in great demand. In the future it will be, but how far that future may be away is anyone's guess. In the meantime much valuable work may be lost when interests change or an unguarded hoard of cassettes is discovered by a child or uncaring member of the family. I would suggest that the best resting place for your work is the local museum or library where such items can be stored and filed with the care and attention they deserve, ready for their future use. It may sometimes be possible to persuade a local authority to sponsor your efforts and in such situations it is understandable that they will expect you to hand over at least taped copies of your results.

Whatever campaign or conflict you will turn your recording efforts to you will be doing a project which future generations will have good reason to thank you for. What is today's mundane gossip is tomorrow's priceless archive. What would a modern historian give for an eye-witness taped account of the Battle of Waterloo? The modern military archaeologist must think in those terms as seen in such a perspective the recording of the voices of war can then be seen as a task of major importance.

Chapter 10

Books, photographs and ephemera

'War! I must write me memoirs!' (Milligan)

Any mention of military archaeology must go hand in hand with books. Books are the source, the end product and very often the bulk of the work involved. No matter what branch of military archaeology you will get involved in, books will be inseparable companions but a considerable number of people have found that books alone can be a subject in themselves. For me there is nothing more pleasant to behold than my own bookshelves with my own favourite volumes that I have amassed over the years—when I am away from them I miss them.

The 20th Century has seen not only an increase in mass violence but an explosion in basic literary skills. As more and more of the world's population has learned to read so has there grown a new industry to supply the literature for their needs. The huge increase in the number of books available to all has not been devoted to purely academic literature but has also involved ever-increasing numbers of purely instructional and educational works and it is in this latter category that most of the books covered in this section will fall. For the main part, the books that the dedicated military archaeologist will be searching after are source works—not the completed histories and compendiums. Any historian will have any number of those at his disposal, but what he will be after is the raw material of history from which opinions and deductions can be drawn.

But a look at the already-published histories will not go amiss. Both World Wars have been recorded in what seems to be an ever-growing number of supposed 'definitive histories', but the truth of the matter is that very often the true histories have yet to be written. The authors of many works were either too involved in events or have been too influenced by contemporary opinion to take the completely detached view of events that is necessary for the true historian. It is for this reason that only now are the events and course of World War 1 being seen in a true historical perspective. World War 2 is still too recent for a correct assessment to be taken and for several reasons the real story behind many of the major events and campaigns cannot be discovered as too many secrets remain uncovered. Only in the last few years, to quote but one example, has the general public become aware of the importance of the *Enigma* decoding machine to Allied planning and strategy between 1939 and 1945. For much of the war the use of this machine enabled the Allies to read and use a great deal of the everyday German war plans and its effect on Allied effort was tremendous. Its importance was so great that many of the already published war histories will have to be re-written one day, including most of the otherwise superb HMSO histories. *Enigma* apart there are doubtless many other factors of which the would-be historian is unaware, and some of these factors may not come to light for many years yet.

This is where the military archaeologist comes in for it is his task to try and

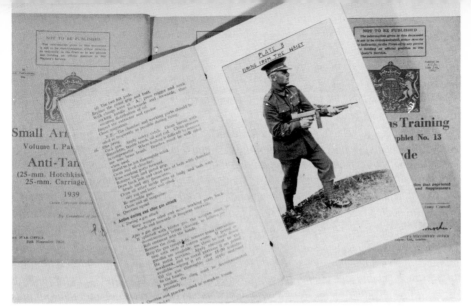

Above and below *The raw material of research. British weapon training manuals as used during World War 2.*

uncover and preserve as much information as possible. Very few of us will be able to discover any matters of great moment but the gradual accumulation of quantities of bits and pieces can help to piece together a true picture just as well as one find of great importance. Every military archaeologist can help in this task for although the historical raw material is still with us now, it may not be around in, say, 50 years' time.

The term 'books' covers a wide field. I will use it to include manuals, magazines, diaries, journals and newspapers. For much of this section I can probably do no more than quote the example of my own particular interest which is the weapons of the two wars. A great deal has been written on the subject and there are several very good books on the subject already on the market. But my interest has gone so far that I still need to go back to the original source material and that means the service manuals issued to the troops who used the weapons at the time they were in service. Searching for these old manuals is a labour of love and a very lengthy one too. Old bookshops have turned up a few but most of my little collection has come from personal contacts, mainly servicemen who had forgotten they still had their old manuals stuck away in cupboards and desks. Very often the facts and figures mentioned in these service manuals are at variance with published data but as the original weapons can rarely be examined (have you ever tried to discover the whereabouts of a British 3-inch mortar which can be examined today?) reliance has to be placed on the manual. But not only the weapon data must be discovered. Just as important is the manner in which it was used, and the drill books are necessary. Once again, the reason for any particular drill must be discovered and the appropriate training manuals must be perused to determine the training philosophy in use at any particular time. An example might make this last point more clear. In 1939 British anti-tank gun tactics were to use the anti-tank gun as a form of relatively static defence. By 1945 that role had been changed into a more mobile attacking one, and not only had the guns changed in size and calibre but the drills and training had been drastically revised.

Further reading is necessary to determine the circumstances in which any particular weapon was used and then regimental, corps and campaign histories have to be consulted. But once again it is better still to consult the original material from which the 'official' histories were compiled. These materials vary a great deal but the unit war diary was often one of the original sources used. This war diary was a day-to-day record of the activities and administrative details of every military formation wherever it was and whatever it was doing. It was the task of an officer in each unit, usually the adjutant or intelligence officer, to make entries in the war diary every day, and sometimes more often if there was anything worth recording. Very often these diaries were just a collection of odd sheets of paper thrown together or a series of signal forms. Needless to say the standards of recording ability varied enormously and all too often a tremendous feat of arms was reduced to the bland level of 'Attack on Hill 529 successful'. These war diaries were not meant to be the sole record for copies were sent back to the regimental or corps depot where they were usually transcribed into more readable documents.

This recording system was used with little variance by all the nationalities involved in both World Wars and many of these diaries can still be consulted in corps and regimental libraries and institutes. Of course, many of the originals were lost or damaged but a surprising number still survive. In the United Kingdom many of the corps and regimental institutes have vanished in the welter of regimental reorganisations carried out since 1945, but very often a 'parent' regiment still keeps the records and opens them for inspection. As an extra some records can be perused at the Public Record Office but it would be as well to enquire whether or not your particular interest is on file there before you go—not all records are held there and much still remains to be sorted and filed. As always, one thing you must do is make an appointment to visit any corps or regimental library well in advance and let them know exactly what you are looking for. That way the staff can be ready for you— many establishments have only limited staff and facilities and if you just turn up expecting them to drop everything to help you, you will be most unpopular.

Apart from their official records many corps and regimental libraries own some personal diaries and journals of men who served with them. Officially, keeping such diaries was usually forbidden but nevertheless many such personal reminders were kept and often they are invaluable sources of information, especially about the sense and spirit of a period. Many old soldiers still retain their old personal diaries but all too often they are thrown away by the uncaring at the earliest opportunity. Any military archaeologist must do all in their power to ensure such personal records are preserved. If you yourself are unwilling to retain such a personal item as a diary the best thing you can do is offer it to the appropriate regimental library—they will usually jump at the chance to obtain such valuable archive material.

One of the main hazards encountered with a great number of old books, magazines and the like is that the materials from which they were assembled were rarely of good quality. In any war the supply of good qualities of wood pulp (the raw material for paper) was near the bottom of shipping priority lists and consequently much of the paper used in wartime was made from whatever was available. Usually

Books such as these can provide first-class research material, not only on facts and figures but they can also be good sources of modelling plans and illustrations. The Handbook on the left is for the Great War 18 pr, while the book on the right, dealing with fire control instruments and dated 1914, was for a long time the standard work on the subject with the British and Empire armies.

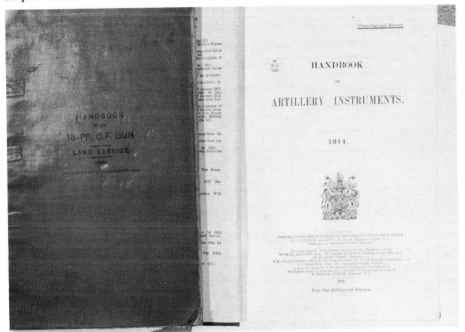

that meant recycled waste paper and rags as the raw materials. The end product was often rough and of low strength. Time is not kind to such a product and over the years such low-quality paper will become discoloured and brittle. Anyone who has handled German wartime publications will know exactly what I mean and all too often such paper will simply disintegrate at a touch. Thus to retain the valuable material that wartime publications often contain, the pages will have to be copied before it is too late.

There are several methods of doing this. The ideal would be to microfilm the material but this can be an expensive process requiring specialised cameras and reading equipment. Although it might be regarded as cheap when compared to other methods of copying, microfilming is out of the question for most of us. But almost anyone who has to consult centralised records will come into contact with microfilm at some time as many large authorities and libraries have had to take recourse to it for the simple reasons of cost and lack of bulk storage. Whole libraries can be placed on a very few reels of microfilm and already many military information agencies have taken this step. Microfilm readers are usually fairly simple to use but the most useful types are those which incorporate a print feed-out device. If any particular frame is wanted for later reference all that is needed is the push of a button and out comes a copy. All very convenient but all too often outside the cost range of most of us.

The camera can still be used as a personal recording medium at a relatively low cost if 35 mm litho film and a simple copy stand are used. Many researchers I know use this recording system not only for storing their information but as an insurance against damage or loss by fire, or any other cause. Most collectors or researchers have at least a few irreplaceable items in their information files and to have such items on a film file is a great reassurance. Some people I know go the extent of placing their back-up negatives in bank deposit boxes but most will not feel the need to go to that extent. All that is usually necessary is to put the negatives in a metal container in a safe place. Almost any 35 mm camera can be used for such copying and the necessary close-up lens attachments are usually quite inexpensive. If you can't run to a copy stand a little ingenuity can be called into play. A cheap tripod and photoflood lamps plugged into ordinary lampholders will often be all that is required. One well-known author uses a small 35 mm hand-held camera and a small flashgun to record any particular page he needs. Costs can be further reduced if you can carry out your own film processing and printing.

Without a doubt the most convenient copying method is to use one of the many types of photocopying machines now on the market. Almost any one of these can deliver an exact facsimile of almost any document within a few seconds. A bewildering array of types and models can be encountered but most fall into two categories—those that copy on to sensitised paper (rather like a photographic plate but positive instead of negative) and those that copy direct onto ordinary paper. The best are those which copy on to ordinary paper as all too often the sensitised paper copiers use a medium which is bulky, sometimes smelly and all too often a degree of impermanence is encountered. A good plain-paper copier has the advantage that very often the copy is as good, if not better than the original and it will never fade. But with both processes cost is a drawback. Each copy will cost you at least 5p and usually a great deal more, for the machines are often leased or hired and each copy is recorded on a meter. This alone will prevent many from making large-scale use of photocopiers. There are relatively cheap copying machines on the market which are quite small and can be used in the home with no trouble at all, but they all use quite expensive sensitised papers and they very often require considerable skill to obtain a good copy. The next decade will probably see a gradual lowering of the costs of photocopying but at present, if you must use a commercial photocopying facility, make sure you can afford it.

A word must be said at this stage about copyright. Copying from books and magazines, whether by camera or photocopier, is a bit of a legal jungle. In law anyone who copies from a published work has to pay a fee to the author or owner of that work. In practice this is usually waived when only a single copy is required for use by only one person, but be very careful how the information copied is used. If it is used verbatim and unchanged in any article or book the law of copyright applies and fees may be exacted. At present copyright applies for only 50 years (which means it covers all World War 2) and some public records are not covered by copyright at all. At present the copyright laws are under considerable public discussion, especially regarding authors' fees for copied books and books borrowed from public libraries and the like, and so changes in copyright procedure may be with us soon. The only advice I can offer is that if you are copying in bulk from published works, assume that copyright applies and take advice from someone who knows more about the subject than I do.

Copying can not only be used to prolong the life of the written word, it can also be used to preserve photographs. Photographs are very much a product of modern times and the military archaeologist will encounter them in almost every field of research. As a pictorial recording medium it is unparalleled but all too often the end product, the photographic print itself, is easily damaged and prone to fading. Despite this the military archaeologist will soon amass a considerable pile of photographs, be they official photographs or personal records. There are some magnificent official collections in being—the Imperial War Museum must be regarded as one of the biggest and best for they hold literally millions of prints and negatives. Elsewhere there are large official collections such as those held by the German *Bundesarchiv*, the French *E.C. Armées*, the massive official files of the US Army and many others, right down to the unique photographic records of the States of Jersey and Guernsey. Prints can be bought from almost all these official collections and they can be held and used for whatever purposes any researcher might wish, that is, apart from publishing them. In almost every case a reproduction fee will be imposed and almost inevitably clearance and permission to publish will also have to be sought. The law of copyright applies to photographs just as much as to published works.

Apart from the official collections the military archaeologist will often discover single photographs or collections belonging to individuals. Combat photographs rarely come into this category but many people in both major wars did manage to take their own particular record of events and journeys and still hidden away in private photograph albums and in odd corners there are some priceless records. All too often such relics have been thrown away, and even when such items come to light the original negatives have been lost. The negative is usually the weakest part of the photographic recording system as it is so easily damaged. Whether on glass or on film, negatives need only a scratch or chemical stain to render them useless so very often the print is all there is to show and use.

The trouble, as stated above, is that prints are often almost as impermanent as the negative. They can be torn, creased or dog-eared and as they rely on a chemical process in the first place, chemical action can, in time, render them useless. The only course open to the archaeologist or collector is to copy any old and interesting prints as soon as possible. Once again this can be an expensive process, especially if the task is given to commercial concerns. The equipment used to copy photographs is not cheap but the average researcher can often produce quite good results with modest equipment. I have gradually compiled a collection of weapon negatives over the last few years using only a cheap copy stand fitted with photoflood lamps, and a 35 mm camera fitted with close-up lenses. (The same equipment can just as easily be used to photocopy documents.) The technique is fairly simple. The photograph to be copied is placed on the stand baseboard and the lights are arranged to ensure no reflections will appear on the negative—a reflex camera is useful here but it is not essential. The camera position is altered to get as much of the photograph in the frame as possible (the larger the negative size the better the quality of the resultant print) and the copy shot is then made. I prefer to use a fairly small 'f' stop to increase the depth of field to cover any slight variations in the distance of the original from the lens—prints rarely lie dead flat unless they are pinned or weighted down but in both

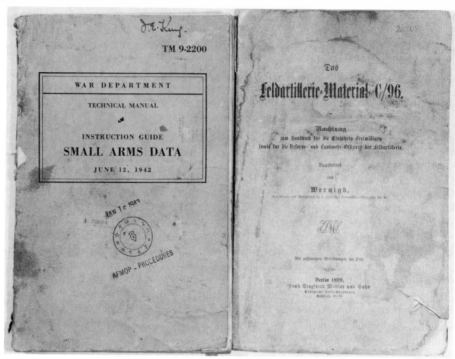

Not only British books can provide a rich mine of information. On the right is the German handbook for the German 77 mm C/96 field gun as used between 1914 and 1918. The American book on the left is a listing of all the American small arms in service in 1942.

cases this might intrude on to the negative. The negatives are then processed in the normal way and the resultant printing uses no unusual techniques. The only things I do not economise on are the quality of the chemicals used, likewise the paper. I never use any chemical unless it is fresh or freshly mixed and I never use cheap or outdated printing paper. The end product has to remain around for a long time if the efforts involved are to be worthwhile. Any attempt to cut costs will often result in an inferior product, namely the print.

Storage of photographs and books can be quite a problem. As mentioned elsewhere any researcher or collector will very soon gather around himself an absolute mass of paper. The photograph problem is usually fairly easily solved, unless you have a collection to rival that of the Imperial War Museum. The answer there is to keep only the negatives until you actually need a print. A negative album together with its indexing system need occupy only a relatively small space and for me the handiest place to keep both is on my bookshelves.

Bookshelves or bookcases can be quite an expensive proposition especially if, like me, your book collection becomes a major end in itself. In no time at all what was originally an odd corner or wall space will soon be filled to overflowing, and if you wish to prevent books taking over the rest of your house some form of racking will be needed. Every individual will have to find his own solution to this problem. If your purse is deep the answer might be with one of the many forms of adjustable wall rack that are on the market. More modest sums will buy a form of industrial racking system which can be adapted to an individual's need, but perhaps the easiest way out is to knock up the shelves yourself from whatever materials are handy. From my own experience the bookcase with closeable and lockable doors is perhaps the best form of book storage but they can be very expensive and they often have the added disadvantage of being relatively inflexible for various book sizes, a disadvantage not shared by flexible racking.

Whatever system you adopt bear in mind the relative conditions in the room. Paper will readily absorb moisture to the extent of ruin but an atmosphere which is too dry will render paper brittle. Extremes of heat and cold will bring their own hazards but heat will often introduce insect life and then problems really begin. There are numerous cutting and boring insects that thrive on paper. Woodlice and Silverfish can live in just about any household but they will rarely infest books or paper that is stored off the floor. Chemical precautions can be taken against insect life in a library but all that most will need to do is just keep an eye open for scurrying forms when books are moved.

A separate mention should be made of magazines. Almost any activity today has its appropriate magazine devoted to its needs and in the field of military archaeology there are several. Few of them are generally available but most are obtainable through private subscription. One of the most interesting and useful widely published examples is *After the Battle* which specialises in the sites and events of the last two conflicts. Other magazines which make mention of our era are *Airfix Magazine* and *Military Modelling* (incorporating *Battle*). Other magazines publish articles from time to time but there is no space here for such a listing. This sheer bulk of numbers can be yet one more problem when it comes to storage, for even one year's supply of a monthly magazine can be quite weighty and take up rather a lot of space. If you are taking more than one magazine the problem becomes even greater. If you have the space (and a good indexing system to go with it) all well and good but many of us are not so fortunate. My own experience has taught me just to remove the pages or articles that are germane to my interests and get rid of the rest. Most magazines seem to take up quite a bit of space with advertisements alone—if those are ditched the space and weight saving can be considerable. My own method is to file away the removed articles and pages in loose-leaf or box files under the various headings—in time I shall try to build up a system of cross-headings.

Ephemera

Over the last five years or so there has been a minor boom in one aspect of the collecting hobbies and that has been the growth of interest in ephemera. The dictionary definition of ephemera mentions 'anything transitory or short-lived' but it has been expanded slightly by collectors into covering virtually anything that is not covered by any other collector's activity. It has a military branch and it is still a small interest but it is growing.

To give examples of what collecting ephemera entails is not easy. I have several bits and pieces in my assembly of militaria that would seem to come under no other heading. They include old mess bills, postcards showing the Home Guard on parade in a local village, amendment sheets for manuals and other such bits and pieces. I suppose you could include such items as identity cards, meal tickets, ration cards, NAAFI entertainment tickets, and bills and receipts. The list could be endless but I find such things to be fascinating. An old mess receipt or manual amendment often has a unit handstamp and a signature and I often wonder who these little scraps of paper were made out to and by whom they were issued. It is remarkable how often such items have survived. Many of mine have been found tucked away in old books and manuals.

Ephemera are not likely to provide the really serious military archaeologist with any great finds or articles of moment but they can provide a sense of period and atmosphere that few other relics can. I shall do my best to add as many little items to my modest collection as opportunity allows.

Notes on Intelligence Reports

This section cannot be complete without an extended mention of one facet of the literature of warfare that no researcher or historian can avoid, namely the use of the various kinds of intelligence reports.

The use of intelligence in war is as old as warfare itself and the two World Wars produced intelligence services that rivalled anything that had gone before, both in size and importance. The intelligence services were charged with the discovery of almost any aspect of the enemy's activities, strengths, equipment and organisation, to say nothing of their intentions. As the scale of warfare grew, so did the power and activities of the intelligence activities, culminating in the large-scale employment of the 'Ultra' secret, based on the previously mentioned 'Enigma' decoding machine which gave the Allied Chiefs of Staff daily information on the German Order of Battle and intentions. Along with this growth in size and scope came an increase in the amount of intelligence information available to soldiers at all levels, and it is these sources that the researcher will find himself coming into contact with time and again.

For all nations the systems of information gathering varied in detail but not in general methods. A comprehensive study of intelligence gathering methods would fill this book but a few general principles will give the basic ideas. Front-line intelligence came from watching the enemy's activities, questioning prisoners-of-war and the like. More information came from agents established behind the lines, resistance workers and partisans. A little, and usually only a little despite some remarkable coups, came from the secret service-type agent, so beloved of popular fiction writers. More came from a constant and careful watch and decoding of enemy radio transmissions, both on the battlefield and at higher levels, and the compiling of information from neutral sources.

The great mass of information so gathered then went to various levels of the intelligence staffs who sifted and sorted it all until a coherent picture emerged. When anything new or important came to light it was disseminated to the appropriate 'customers' who then decided to pass it further or await more information. Again, the practices differed from nation to nation but what usually happened was that weekly intelligence bulletins were issued at several levels (the intervals varied sometimes). The levels reflected the different state of knowledge at any one time. Brand-new information was issued in typed or hastily set-up printed sheets to the higher staff echelons only. Information which had been more fully established or confirmed went to the medium levels such as Corps and divisional HQs and the fully substantiated (and cleared) information sometimes went down as far as Company level. By the time it got to the soldier in the field information on such things as enemy equipment, uniforms and tactics was presented in what was very often an attractive illustrated booklet form, intended for reference and general reading material.

It is usually only the latter two types of intelligence information that the general historian or researcher will come into contact with. I am perhaps better qualified to comment on the British side of things as it is with them that I have personally had most experience. The medium level of information was usually issued in weekly bulletins which were often typed and run-off on off-set printing machines. If illustrations were included, they were usually line drawings transcribed from photographs, but by 1944 more and more actual photographs were included. I have had most experience with the technical literature but tactical and other bulletins were similar. Most of these bulletins were issued as far down as battalion level and thus many have survived. However, those that went higher were usually lost to view or have yet to be released, but they can be found in some regimental or Corps libraries.

Needless to say, some of the wartime bulletins were often wrong and subsequent issues sometimes made the necessary corrections, but not always. Thus the researcher has to use them with caution and often in conjunction with other material. Over the years I have learned not to trust them implicitly and, with all due respect, some of the American bulletins have proved to be widely erroneous—but the same can be said of many German sources, and some of the World War 1 British bulletins now appear to have been fictional.

Perhaps the most reliable material to use is the variety which filtered down to Company level as by the time it got that far the true facts were usually pretty well established and reliable. Some of these have proved to be so good that today they have been thought worthy of reprinting and publishing commercially. A good example from the Great War is the *German Army Handbook, April 1918*, available from Arms and Armour Press, which is a valuable goldmine of information. World War 2 produced many other bulletins that are commercially available today. Arms and Armour Press have issued the *German Order of Battle 1944* while the American Normount concern have brought out a long string of American Intelligence

When the Home Guard was first formed in 1940 they lacked all sorts of equipment including training material. As a result they provided their own and the more successful exponents had their work published. This picture shows just a few of them and, as can be seen, the novelist John Brophy turned his hand to the needs of war.

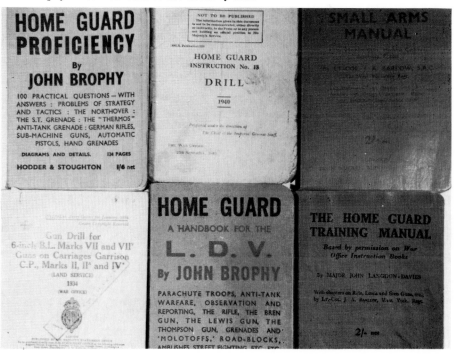

compilations. One is a reproduction of TM-E 30-451 (the E denotes a document relating to an enemy topic) which is titled *Handbook on German Military Forces* and dated March 1945. It is still the best book of its type that I have seen, and the same firm has also issued TM-E 30-480 which deals with the Japanese Armed Forces.

But, in the case of World War 2, these latter publications were the final fruits of activities which began well before 1939. Prior to this date most nations were quietly gathering information on other armies but none more earnestly and successfully than the Germans. By 1939 they had produced masses of data on every nation in Europe (but were less well informed with confirmed facts on forces elsewhere, especially regarding the United States). Some of this information I have been happy to use myself, especially regarding equipment, weapons and artillery. Much of the sorted material was compiled into a series of handbooks known as the D.50 Series, and titled *Kennblätter fremden Geräts*. These were issued from OKH and usually related to army matters while the Luftwaffe and Kriegsmarine published their own counterparts. As pure data sources these books are hard to beat and the researcher will find them very useful—if you can find copies as few now seem to exist.

From time to time the efficient German war machine made very good use of all this intelligence work when they invaded other nations. I have in my modest collection a copy of the *Taschenbuch Jugoslawisches Heer* dated January 1941 (I found it in a Brighton bookshop), which contains information on the Jugoslav Army strength and disposition, its weapons, map markings, information on the country and even a few pages of uniforms and insignia in colour. These little books were issued right down to front-line NCO level and today such sources are invaluable. Of course, many other nations, including our own, were busy collecting and producing similar material but until 1943, at least, the Germans seem to have had the edge on the Allies. After that date things went the other way and frequently the front-line Allied soldier had information on German weapons before the German troops were issued with them! The American Army went to the extent of bringing out handbooks on German weapons for their own troops to use if they captured any, a practice they often had to resort to in late 1944 when the advancing armies in Europe outstripped their own supply lines. One such book I have seen is TM-E 9-228 which deals with the 2 cm Flakvierling 28, but there were numerous others. On the British side, the front-line troops were frequently issued with updates of *The German Army Illustrated* which was a series of pictorial loose-leaf pages showing all aspects of the German Army and its weapons and equipment. Many of these have survived and can be seen in numerous military libraries.

But contrary to expectation the best intelligence reports were issued well after the war was over. Even as the conflict was in its final and nasty stages intelligence teams from all the Allied nations were busy raking over the ashes of the German depots, factories and barracks. By patient and careful searching they were able to discover all manner of unknown areas of German activity. All too often the investigations were carried out in areas of Germany which were later to come under Soviet domination so the searching frequently took the form of crating masses of documents, tools and equipment back to Allied areas. By the end of 1945 some preliminary reports had been compiled and issued, and these reports are precious indeed. Most were published by the Combined Intelligence Objectives Sub-Committee, or CIOS (not to be confused with the Channel Islands CIOS), which was made up of intelligence officers from all the Western Allied nations.

However, each country also had teams on a national basis who were busy on the same task, and the British equivalent was the British Intelligence Objectives Sub-Committee, or BIOS. The reports first issued by late 1945 provide a fascinating

The author's copying stand. It is a fairly cheap model, and ordinary photofloods have been used in place of the more expensive specialist photocopying lamps. The camera is a simple single-lens reflex with inexpensive close-up lens attachments.

source of all manner of things from coastal defences to small-arms research and development. But they were all too often only intended as preliminaries while the really detailed work went on at an Allied information centre based at Unterluss in the BAOR sector of Germany. There, a team of qualified experts sifted and sorted the great piles of documents, and at Ford Halstead in Kent another unit was busy on many technical projects arising from advanced German development programmes. However, even as late as 1950 there was still much work to be done and by that time the intelligence teams, or what was left of them, were supplying information to no one. The post-1945 reduction of the Western Allied armed forces meant that there was no longer any interested customer to supply, so the sifting operations drew to a gradual close with much original material still in its crates and a great deal of information lost in the huge log-jam of documentation produced by the various intelligence bodies and sub-bodies.

Unfortunately many of these 'late' reports were not very well presented and were typed sheets placed in the flimsy manilla folders favoured by economy-minded bureaucrats the world over. Usually only a few copies were issued so if you can uncover one of these 'late' reports in some dusty archive you will have made a real find.

Fortunately the British War Office did produce a sizeable compilation of the basic facts of several fields of German technical ability in 1945. This project, known as the *Illustrated Record of German Army Equipment 1939-1945* (usually referred to as the IROGs) was commenced in 1947 and five volumes were scheduled as follows: Vol 1—*Infantry Weapons*; Vol 2—*Artillery* (issued in two sections); Vol 3—*Armoured Fighting Vehicles*; Vol 4—*Vehicles* (other than AFVs); and Vol 5—*Mines, Mine Detectors and Demolition Equipment*.

Volume 1 was never completed, or if it was I have never seen a copy. All the others were issued and distributed widely so that today nearly every military library seems to have a copy hidden away somewhere—for the technically minded they will provide a wealth of data. But beware of the AFV volume as it has been used as the basis of several works on German tanks.

As far as I know the Americans did not get round to producing a comparable work. The Canadians cheated a bit and simply compiled a series of technical data sheets based on extracts from service manuals, intelligence bulletins and the like. Again, the results were widely distributed and are not very difficult to find. They are especially invaluable in that they cover Allied equipment as well as Axis. As an extra, each entry is annotated with its reference source which is very useful for later research.

I have concentrated above on the subject I know best, namely the compiling of data from weapon reports and bulletins, but much of it can also relate to other fields of research. After 1945 reports were issued on tactics, uniforms, organisation, and supply of all the Axis forces. Much of it has been available for a long time but still hidden away in old archives and the back corners of libraries. Time spent in searching for them will be well rewarded.

Chapter 11

Photographic interpretation

Another section of this book deals with the collecting, care and copying of old military photographs, but this chapter will give a few pointers as to how to use them to discover more than they, at first, appear to show. This feature will *not* deal with the interpretation of vertical aerial photographs of the type taken by photographic reconnaissance aircraft—that is a science all of its own.

The use of photography as a recording or reporting medium began with the early efforts of the Crimean and American Civil War photographers. By 1900 photography was an exact science as far as our period is concerned. The Great War, as well as World War 2, saw an ever-growing number of specialised military photographers, in uniform, doing nothing else but constantly taking photographs which were used as blatant propaganda, for news reports and, when nothing else was happening, for purely recording purposes. To these military photographers can be added the small armies of civilian reporters and photographers, and the even larger numbers of soldiers who carried and used their own cameras. As a general rule soldiers, both in the front line and elsewhere, were not allowed to carry cameras to take photographs but, as any ex-serviceman will tell you, this ruling was frequently ignored. The end result of all this picture-taking is with us still. Mounds and mounds of prints have survived, but many more have been lost, or remain to be discovered. National collections in almost every combatant nation are generally available to the public, but these archives are nearly all the work of the official photographers, both military and civil. They were taken for official purposes and thus tend to show what the authorities wanted them to show—and no more.

This is where the art of photographic interpretation comes in, for the modern historian and researcher will have to use these official photographs in nearly every sphere of his work. Sooner or later you will come across photographs which purport to show certain things but in fact are otherwise. Very often the background of a photograph will reveal more than the main subject in the foreground. The researcher should be constantly on the lookout for such things. Having had a little experience in looking at many thousands of photographs I have listed below a few pointers which will be useful to others, especially those new to the field.

One factor always to bear in mind when examining photographs is that they are very rarely prints taken from original negatives. Consequently all sorts of things might have happened to them. For a variety of reasons, prints and negatives can be retouched to hide detail or enhance the tones of the picture to improve reproduction. By the same token, backgrounds can be obliterated or even altered so that the foreground subject, for example a vehicle, can be made to appear in an entirely different setting—many propaganda-type photographs suffer from this. So beware of the picture that has large areas of single tones or which shows trees and shrubs with unnaturally rounded foliage. After even a little practice such things become obvious and the photograph can then be treated with the suspicion it deserves.

The copying and recopying of prints and negatives also brings another unwanted feature and that is lack of quality and definition on the final print. If you can, try to obtain as early a print as possible from a negative so that much of the fine detail remains. Here a small magnifying glass is useful, although it does not need to be very powerful.

It is extremely difficult to determine shades of colour accurately from a black-and-white print so, unless you are really practiced and skilled in the art, don't try it and state your results as historical truths. The same can be said of some early colour photography when shades of yellow turned out to be mauve on the finished print. If you must make a stab at a colour shade try to look for some part of the print which you definitely know is a certain shade and then compare it with the mystery colour. But it is impossible to come to definite conclusions here.

Try not to take pictures on their face value and if there are any dates on the back, as there are with some old agency or official prints, always treat them with suspicion. The same goes for captions which were often altered to suit the mood of the moment or fill a need. I have frequently seen one particular picture of troops on a half-track which has been used to describe the Germans entering Warsaw, Prague or Paris—take your pick. The answer can only be ascertained by close examination, and even then the full truth may be impossible to discover. However, a suprising amount can be revealed from even the most innocent-looking prints and the best way to give examples of this is to include a few 'case histories'.

Case history 1. A quick glance would tend to write this print off as yet another run-of-the-mill Western Desert picture. But look a bit closer. Those soldiers not in steel helmets are wearing French officer-style peaked hats. Straight away we have discovered that at least some of the soldiers are Free French and so the picture is more unusual than at first thought. What about the troops in the truck; are they Free French too? They are wearing British uniforms which was not unusual in North

Africa among some French units, but the sight of a Hotchkiss machine-gun barrel poking over the tailboard would confirm that they are indeed French as no other nation used this weapon in North Africa. A closer look at the uniforms under the French hats reveals French-style greatcoats and belt pouches, so the wearers might have been based in Morocco or Tunisia, but the background would indicate the latter. The truck has the general appearance of a Chevrolet, but bears a minor mystery in the shape of the heart symbol which I am unable to identify.

Case history 2. The date on this picture, which has only a bland agency caption, is August 28 1941, but that was the date it was passed by the censor for publication and the real date must have been well before that. So here we have a good example for some detective work. The tractor vehicle is a variation of an AEC 6 × 6 fitted with a small crane jib—the sand channels on the side are a nice extra touch. The vehicle being towed is a Cruiser Tank Mark III which straight away puts the date at around 1941 as it was a model which proved to be too lightly armed and armoured for service after the end of that year. The tank bears the white rhinoceros in a black oval symbol of the 1st Armoured Division which did not arrive in the Middle East until early 1941 which would tend to confirm the date. The crew are all wearing solar topees as are several other foreground figures which would mark them as newly arrived 'sprogs', for the tractor driver is wearing a far more serviceable cap. The tractor has a rather unusual number plate marked 1500 in black on a white plate, and just visible underneath (with a glass) is 'W.D.'. This is not a common British Army marking so the tractor might have come from Egyptian Army stocks.

3

Case history 3. This rather poor-quality photograph (the result of its being a copy of a copy of a copy . . .) bears no date or caption but the troops and vehicles are obviously German. The problem is where or when? I cannot be certain but my guess is Poland in the winter of 1944-45—more than that is impossible to say. My assumption is based on the Schützen side plates on most of the AFVs visible—they started to come into service around 1942—but what dates it later than that is the Panther partly hidden behind the cross head. A glass is needed to sort out the recognition shapes, even though the long gun is a give-away—thus it is post-1943. But it is the cross itself which shows the area is not Russia even though the background indicates Eastern Europe. The Germans were not pushed back into Poland until late 1944 and as there is snow on the ground . . .

Case history 4. Another mystery photograph with no caption or date. A quick look indicates French soldiers but closer study shows this is not so. The troops are Belgian. For a start the helmets are different and the carbine to be seen on the left is a Mauser model, a type definitely not used by the French. The non-artillery buff is excused for not recognising the gun itself for it is a Canon de 47 antichars SA-FRC, a

4

weapon produced in Belgium for the Belgian Army alone. The exact date cannot be determined but the general style and layout of the photograph is pre-1939. If the gun had been emplaced for any warlike purpose other than manoeuvres or posed as a publicity shot the soldiers would be anywhere but around the gun, because in action they would easily have been wiped out in the first burst of enemy fire. Why so many are shown is revealed by the carrying handles protruding from under the gun itself. Manhandling even such a small artillery piece would have been no easy task.

Case history 5. Following on from the previous example this photograph reveals that the tendency for soldiers to cluster around guns is nothing new but it is possible to give this picture an approximate date. I would put it at around 1900-1901 for the reason that there *is* such a cluster around the gun. By 1900 the British had learned the hard way that a group of gunners behind an artillery piece made a good target for the devastingly accurate long-range Boer rifle fire, and began to fit shields to their guns while at the same time reducing the number of gunners serving their pieces. The Germans had observers in South Africa and were quick to follow such minor tactical changes. These guns (they are 7.7 cm FK 96s) have only rudimentary

5

shields which were later enlarged, while the number of men on the gun was later reduced to around four, all of whom were kneeling. The number on the helmets is 55 which reveals them to be from the 2. Thüringisches Feldartillerie-Regiment Nr.55 based at Naumberg. The uniforms would have been blue.

Case history 6 (overleaf). Well, here it is, the very stuff of legend—the British parachutist's folding bike! Released for publication on November 12 1943, this photograph gives as much detail as is needed, including the pump stowage. It is even possible to discover where it was made as a close look at the main drive gear will reveal the letters BSA. It is a pity that the soldier's cap badge is not shown (probably deliberately). Apart from its technical interest, this picture will remind people of one of the most famous jokes of World War 2. It concerned a parachutist whose parachute did not open. Just before he hit the ground he was heard to remark, 'And I bet the folding bike don't work either!'

Case history 7. This odd little picture poses more questions than its caption answers. It purports to show American troops moving up to the front through Avola in Sicily. Well, it certainly looks like Sicily with the noon-day sun and the style of architecture, but the troops don't look very warlike and neither does their transport. Despite the pile of personal equipment on the back of the donkey cart the driver is hardly prepared for action. Another odd twist is the machine-gun in the trailer. At first glance it looks like a Browning but a look through a magnifying glass reveals it to be an Italian Mitraglice Breda modello 37—hardly a standard weapon for American forces. But the possible solution lies with the carbine carried by the walking figure. It has a very thin butt and is thus a Carbine, Calibre .30 M1A1—a weapon usually

issued to airborne formations. As the Sicily invasion featured one of the first American airborne operations a lot of gliders and troops ended up in the sea together with all the heavy equipment—thus a captured enemy weapon would have been very welcome.

8

Case history 8. No caption, no date but obviously taken on a training range somewhere. What looks wrong with the 17 pdr anti-tank gun in the foreground is that the trail spades aren't dug in as they would be if the gun had fired even a few rounds. Peering through a glass the answer can be seen over the barrel for on it is perched a Bren Gun, obviously being used as a sub-calibre training device, even if it doesn't have a magazine fitted. The reason for such an arrangement can hardly be range restrictions for the 6 pdrs in the background show no such fittings. A more likely solution was that a temporary ammunition shortage prompted the fitting of the Bren Gun as a training aid. The wheels are not the same as those fitted to most production models and thus it may be that this is an early service prototype being used to determine gun drills. By the way, I bet the range is on the Yorkshire Moors not far from Catterick.

Case history 9. Again, no caption and no date. This picture has long been in my collection and until recently I have just glanced at it and thought 'Sturmgeschütz 40'. But a closer look soon reveals that it isn't, for it's a Sturmgeschütz M 42 mit 75/34 (851) (i), an Italian assault gun used by German formations based in Italy after 1943. The divisional sign cannot be identified from my own references but the

9

tactical sign (the trapezoid) denotes the vehicle belongs to a battalion commander. The positioning of the assault gun looks a bit odd, but what has more than likely happened is that the commander has situated it to fire in ambush through a window or embrasure at the front of the vehicle.

Case history 10. This is the sort of photograph that annoys many historians. It is dated 1943 and purports to depict a mobile Bofors AA gun ready to move. Well, it shows a Bofors all right but that is about the only part of the caption which is correct. The picture is obviously posed and several things look very wrong. If the gun is supposed to be ready to move why are there no covers in sight, and why are there

10

rounds loaded and ready to hand? Why are there two gun numbers still in their aiming seats (when they should be on the tractor), and why is the rest of the detachment seated on the roof? If that isn't enough the gunners are posed with their hands on the training gear while the barrel is held fast in its clamp. To add insult to injury the censor has seen fit to obliterate all markings on the tractor apart from the serial number which won't tell us very much. All in all, a very unsatisfactory illustration which tells us little apart from some gun detail.

11

Case history 11. This one is still a mystery and is dated July 1942. The centre-piece is a gun which I cannot identify, but I would lay money that it is situated at Shoeburyness, one of the main artillery experimental establishments, despite the efforts of the censor to hide the background buildings. The gun is like nothing I have ever seen in any modern textbook, and looks as though it is an experimental model from a past era. Note how the traversing sector on the ground is limited despite the fact that it is obviously intended to be a coast defence gun—perhaps this was a safety measure. The davits on the rear of the gun show no sign of pulley cables which might indicate dis-use. The soldier is obviously a Royal Artillery Battery Sergeant Major or AIG, but note the large jack-knife worn by the ATS girl. Returning to the gun note the lack of recoil cylinders. The recoil system seems to have been based on the sliding ramp method, a technique which went out of favour in the late 19th Century.

Case history 12. How not to do it. These American troops are supposed to be demonstrating the use of captured German anti-tank weapons and the soldier in the foreground is holding a Panzerfaust 60 fairly correctly. But the man at the back is totally wrong. He is supposed to be launching a Panzerwurfmine but his action is incorrect. This odd anti-tank grenade was intended for throwing by its folded fabric

vanes in the manner of throwing a bolas. The odd thing is that this mistaken launching method was carried into some 1944 intelligence bulletins and was not corrected for some time. Once again the maxim has to be: don't believe every picture as being the gospel truth—check it out.

The above examples can give only a small idea of the scope of correct photographic interpretation, and I have no doubt that some of my conclusions will be thought or proved incorrect—indeed many will question my methods and assumptions. But if it does nothing else I hope it will increase the reader's awareness of what can be deduced from pictorial sources. All the examples I have given have come from official or semi-official sources. Just think of how much more there is to be found from pictures taken by individuals without official knowledge or consent. At the time such pictures might have been considered security risks—today they may be valuable sources of historical information.

Chapter 12

Weapons

Considering the violent course of the 20th Century to date one cannot but wonder at the fact that the human race has survived at all, such has been the huge increase in weapon lethality. Weapons, in all their diversity, have been increased in efficiency and availability over the last one hundred years to the extent that they alone have often dictated political and social events, but somehow the world has learned to live with the fact. For this reason alone weapons have a great interest to the military archaeologist, to say nothing of the fascination that they have for many people, a fascination which has nothing to do with the destructive powers of weapons themselves.

But the sad thing is that many military archaeologists, especially those who confine themselves to the years since 1900, will never be able actually to own a modern weapon of their own. The ever-increasing military violence of our times has spilled-over into the everyday social sphere to the extent that nowadays most nations have been forced to impose severe degrees of restriction on those who own or carry weapons of nearly every description. Very often this legislation prohibits even the ownership of many types of weapon and, although understandable, firearms in all their forms are strictly controlled to the extent that many will never have an example to call their own. In the United Kingdom a private person may own a firearm provided he can show a lawful reason to do so but the authorities are very often reluctant to grant a firearms licence to anyone who wishes to own guns for their historical interest alone. Even museums that display firearms have to render them useless before they can go on public show and even then strict security precautions have to be taken.

All categories of firearms have to be licensed in the United Kingdom and their storage in premises of any kind is strictly controlled and supervised. Some categories of firearm, such as automatic weapons, are quite simply not even entertained for public ownership and the penalties for infringement are severe. Some parts of the United Kingdom, such as the Channel Islands, do allow collectors to amass automatics but they are extremes and the end result is that many who would love to own a few examples of the guns that were carried by the soldiers of two World Wars will never be able to do so.

There are a few ways round this state of affairs but they are not easy and will be beyond the resources of many. One way to own a military rifle is to purchase an example that has had its rifling removed by boring out to a shotgun calibre—usually .410. But even this rather extreme measure requires the ownership of a shotgun certificate and in many parts of the United Kingdom these are becoming increasingly difficult to obtain. At the time of writing even stricter shotgun legislation seems likely and very soon the bored-out rifle may be a thing of the past. At the present time these hybrids are not cheap and the cost of even a mediocre sample of a No 4 Mark 1 Lee-Enfield rifle is likely to be around £50—well outside the financial range of those other than the well-heeled. Add to this the high costs of keeping such a weapon in a legally secure place or cabinet and the shotgun/rifle becomes a very expensive proposition.

Firearms are not the only weapons controlled by law for at the time of writing edged weapons have many strictures imposed on them. Again, these restrictions are understandable but they do prevent amateur historians from carrying out their activities with the freedom they would like. Such items as trench and fighting knives, along with bayonets and swords, can be bought and sold but they may not be carried in a public place and anyone wishing to display them would do well to consult their local police force to see how they would react to such a situation. In many cases the Police, who have the unenviable task of administering the bulk of United Kingdom weapons legislation, will place few obstacles in the paths of *bona fide* edged weapons collectors but it would be as well to check with them first. But as mentioned above with firearms, the relative costs are often high as edged weapon collecting is now a very popular hobby.

A recent development in the small firearms field has been the emergence of a range of replica firearms. These replicas, usually made in Japan, are now freely available and can be bought by anyone over the counters of model shops and gun shops, or even obtained by mail order and there are no restrictions on ownership or storage. A replica gun is exactly what it says and very often the differences between the replica and the real thing are very difficult to detect. Stripping and handling are usually identical to the original but the big difference is that the replicas are made from die-cast or light alloys and *cannot* be fired. Any attempt to use real ammunition will result in damage and injury and for this reason it is not recommended that even dummy ammunition should be loaded into them—the risk of accident is too high. The attraction of the replica handgun to the collector is often great but many will be put off by the relatively high costs involved in purchasing an example. Prices can be discovered by perusing the advertisements in most modelling or gun magazines but if you wish to buy one it is usually best to examine an example in a shop as the standards of accuracy and appearance vary from make to make and very often it is not always the most expensive product that is the most realistic. A wide range of handguns is now available and there are even replica sub-machine guns on sale. It is salutary to note that in this country the cost of a replica Sten Gun is now over 20 times that of the original produced between 1941 and 1945! But here again the violent times we live in are once more making themselves apparent and many police authorities are taking a long hard look at the open availability of replica guns—in the near future some form of restrictive legislation seems very likely.

With so many restrictions on the ownership of weapons it would seem that it is not an area in which the military archaeologist can become very involved but once more the opposite is true. The historian still has a great deal of work to carry out with the weapons of two World Wars and all the many other conflicts that have taken place since 1900, but very little of it will have to be carried out with the actual weapons themselves. The work that still needs to be done covers a very wide field indeed, from dimensions and weights of the weapons themselves, to the scale of issue, where they were used (and, just as important, *how* they were used), who used them and a whole host of other topics. If empirical data on weights and measures is needed the weapons themselves are, of course, necessary. Very often this can be arranged with many museums and regimental institutes who may hold the items concerned in their collections, but remember that permission and access will usually have to be arranged well in advance. Failing this there are many books and magazines devoted to the weapons field, and very often they contain as much data as the average researcher will ever need, but even better are the service handbooks and manuals issued by the military authorities for the users in the field.

Discovering the dimensions of a weapon is relatively easy when compared with the other research aspects. As mentioned above, finding out where it was issued can be a major task. For example I have yet to discover to what units the de Lisle silent carbine was issued during the 1939-1945 war—vague references to Commandos and Resistance fighters have been found, but to exactly which units and on what scale is still unknown to me—yet that information must be somewhere. Production figures is another area that still requires research, and the grim-sounding 'kill-rate' of many relatively modern weapon types is still a subject which (understandably) requires investigation. Not only infantry small-arms require research—my own particular subject is the artillery of the 1939-1945 war, and it is one that I have found absorbing and rewarding. But it is hardly possible to have my own artillery park in the back garden.

It is nevertheless an established fact that a great number of people who are interested in weapons would also like to collect them (I would love to own a 25 pdr). The restrictions which prevent this are a definite legal block on such activities but I would like to suggest two facets of collecting which can combine an interest in weapons with a subject worthy of further investigation and research. One has been mentioned already, and that is collecting bayonets. The other is a relatively new activity, namely collecting inert small-arms ammunition and I feel it worthy of a separate study.

Inert small-arms ammunition

The ownership of even a single round of small-arms ammunition is an offence under United Kingdom firearms regulations and a firearms certificate is required for even one cartridge. But no such certificate is needed if the round concerned has been rendered inert and over the last few years this has become the basis for one of Britain's fastest-growing collecting activities, namely collecting inert small-arms ammunition. The attraction of such an activity is not difficult to understand as small-arms ammunition has a visual attraction in its own right and another grimmer aspect is that it must not be forgotten that in the gun/ammunition combination it is the projectile which is the weapon—the gun is merely the delivery system. Ever since the projectile and the propellent were joined together in the cartridge there has been an amazing variety of calibres and combinations produced. The original cartridges were usually made with rolled paper but gradually metal took over and by the 1880s the brasscase/bullet combination was well established to the extent that it is still the most common cartridge to be found. Many other metals such as steel and copper have been used and the paper cartridge is still with us for use in shotguns but such variations can only add to the interest.

In its simplest form inert ammunition is just a commercially produced piece of ammunition which has had its propellant removed. This is no easy task as it must be done safely and properly and for the collector it must be done without damaging the cartridge in any way. Needless to say it is not a process which can be carried out in the kitchen and it should not be attempted by anyone who does not know what he is about. The only way to obtain inert ammunition is to buy it from a dealer but fortunately this is not yet an expensive operation. In many ways collecting inert ammunition is in very much the same state as coin collecting was about 25 years ago. Then coin collecting was very much a specialist occupation and good examples were relatively cheap. Today those same examples are prohibitively expensive. Much the same may happen with inert ammunition and today an inert .303 cartridge may be

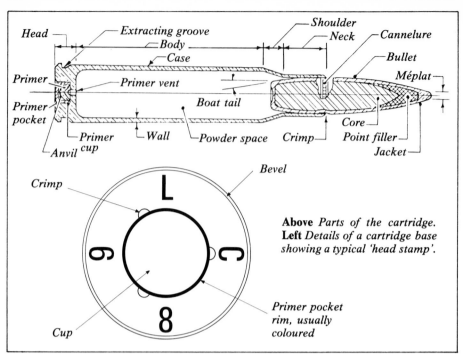

Above *Parts of the cartridge.*
Left *Details of a cartridge base showing a typical 'head stamp'.*

bought for as little as 35p or so. Such were the vast quantities and varieties of .303 cartridges produced that it is possible to build up a sizeable little collection of inert .303 rounds alone for a unit cost of less than £1 an item. Other and rarer rounds can cost more but it is rare to find an item that would cost you more than £10 (at the time of writing) and the bulk of the cartridges available will cost far less than that.

One of the attractions of collecting inert ammunition is the very large range of calibres and types of ammunition available. It would be possible to specialise in just one aspect of the subject such as drill rounds (which require no firearms certificate anyway as they are already inert), armour piercing rounds, rounds made especially for aircraft use, and so on. It is also possible to centralise a collection around one calibre—.303 was mentioned above but it would also be possible to concentrate on the German 7.92 mm or the American .30.

But an inert ammunition collection has an added advantage in that it can form the basis for a great deal of further research. An obvious outlet for this is the weapons from which the ammunition was meant to be fired, but the ammunition itself is often worthy of a great deal of study. Cartridges use a language of their own to differentiate between the various types as the accompanying illustration shows and the many and various head-stamp codes used are an area of study in themselves. The head-stamps can give all manner of information ranging from where and when it was manufactured to the type of propellant used. The projectiles or bullets can also give further information as they are often colour-coded to denote the type of bullet used. Yet another area worthy of study can be considered when the various types of clip or feeder device are encountered, all of which can add to the collection or investigation.

As yet, inert ammunition is a relatively cheap commodity but it may not remain so for very much longer. Already the number of collectors are growing and despite the huge numbers of types and cartridges churned out over the years the supply is not infinite—cartridges were meant to be fired and not collected. Inert ammunition can be used as the starting point for a great deal of weapons research and as the basis for one form of military archaeology. Already some people have built up magnificent collections and many others are delving into the past to discover odd types and other mysteries. A very few people with specialised knowledge and skills have even started to build up collections of inert artillery ammunition but that is one line I would not recommend to anyone as, to put it mildly, it can be a dangerous occupation, and even obtaining the raw materials can be hazardous to all around you. So stick to commercially available inert small-arms ammunition.

For anyone in the United Kingdom who is interested, the best person to contact is Ken Elks who runs Collector Cartridges, postal address Kingston, Canterbury, Kent. If you send him an A4 stamped self-addressed envelope you will receive his current list of items and prices—and fascinating reading it makes too.

Bayonets

Bayonets are another facet of weapon collecting which are within the current law, but it is as well to remember that the public showing of such items should be cleared with your local police force, and wearing or brandishing bayonets in public is most definitely illegal.

One of the military anachronisms of the 20th Century is the retention of the bayonet as a service weapon but for a number of reasons it is still in use—even the recently-unveiled British 4.85 mm Individual Weapon still has provision for a small bayonet. Perhaps the most important reason for its retention is that it is still a superb close-quarter weapon and if nothing else its appearance can often be a most important morale factor. Despite the many modern variations the bayonet has changed little over the centuries and apart from the actual method of fitting to the musket muzzle many modern bayonets would not have been too out-of-place in the Crimea. The bayonets in use between 1914 and 1918 were fearsome-looking things and many of them were still in use between 1939 and 1945 but those same years saw a gradual trend towards simpler and shorter bayonet designs. Perhaps the extreme

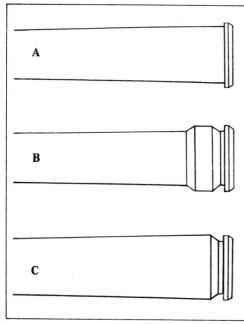

Cartridge types. **A** *Rimmed. This was the type used in the British 0.303 series. While it was a sound principle and provided a good seating for the cartridge in the weapon chamber it had the disadvantage that automatic feeding was rendered more complicated—the cartridge had to be withdrawn backwards from a feeder belt and then pushed forward rather than just pushed forward as was the case with rimless ammunition.* **B** *Semi-rimmed. This principle was adopted for only a few of the heavier small-arms calibres such as the British .55 Boys anti-tank rifle. Seating in the chamber was against the raised band forward of the rim. Relatively few weapons used this principle.* **C** *Rimless. This is the most commonly encountered type of cartridge and it was used for the German 7.92 mm series, both normal and kurz, and for the American 0.30.*

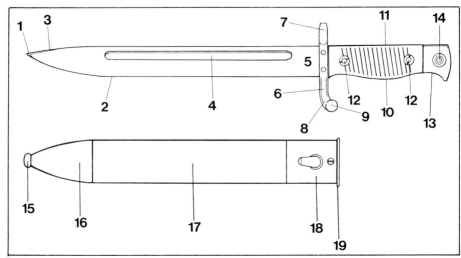

Bayonet terminology
1 *Point*
2 *True edge*
3 *False edge*
4 *Fuller*
5 *Ricasso*
6 *Crosspiece*
7 *Muzzle ring*
8 *Quillon*

9 *Finial*
10,11 *Grips*
12 *Bolts or rivets*
13 *Pommel*
14 *Press stud*
The bayonet shown is a composite one and some features mentioned above will not appear on every

model.
Bayonet scabbard terminology
15 *Finial*
16 *Chape*
17 *Body*
18 *Locket or topmount*
19 *Mouthpiece*
Drawings by Ken Musgrave.

was reached with the short and simple spike bayonet used on the No 4 Mark 1 British rifle but several other earlier designs were as basic.

The truth is that the front-line soldier and the bayonet are old friends. In battle the actual fitting of a bayonet can often be a most reassuring action and the sight of bayonets at the charge can often cause faint hearts to falter. When not in battle the bayonet can be forced into a variety of odd tasks that can vary from preparing a chicken for cooking to opening a locked wardrobe. To the civilian or the collector the bayonet has obvious military connotations and indeed, many of them cannot be used for any peaceful purpose. To the military historian or archaeologist the bayonet can be used to discover a great deal of information regarding the weapon to which it was fitted and the tactical situation in which it was used. An example of this point can be made by a comparison of the long sword bayonet of the No 1 Mark 111* rifle of 1914-1918 with the aforementioned spike bayonet of the No 4 Mark 1. The long sword bayonet was very much a result of the expected hand-to-hand trench and infantry fighting still dominated by the foot soldier. The spike design was a result of the more mobile fluid fighting bought about by modern industrial potential and methods—the spike itself was a manufacturing expedient. This small example can thus demonstrate how a researcher can use the bayonet as a research tool but the bayonet is very much a study in itself. The accompanying illustration shows how, over the years, the bayonet has built up its own terminology. Bayonet collectors are now very much a feature of the militaria scene as any glance at the columns of the *Exchange and Mart* will show.

For the average military archaeologist or enthusiast the bayonet can be a useful and interesting branch of an interest but to collect them these days can be a rather expensive pastime. Even common and well-known items are now fetching high prices and some rarities are fetching prices that put them out of the reach of all but the very dedicated or the very rich. Nevertheless it is still possible to pick up good examples by various means, usually by a chance purchase in a second-hand shop or a lucky discovery in a relative's loft. This is still possible for the reason that since 1900 the bayonet has been produced in millions and they made very convenient souvenirs which were obtained by conquest, swapping or downright theft. Nearly every man in uniform brought one home at some time or other and there must still be many hidden away. Other job lots have appeared on the open market over the years as obsolete rifles, together with their bayonets, were replaced by more modern equipment, and the subsequent swamping of the market can often depress prices (usually for a short time only).

When buying a bayonet there are several things to look for. The most obvious thing is whether or not it has a scabbard. If it does have a scabbard (without one the value is much lower) it should be closely examined to discover if it is the correct type, and if it is, a further and useful refinement is to check the serial numbers. Most bayonets usually (but not always) have a serial number or letter combination stamped somewhere on the blade or cross-piece. If this serial number is the same as that on the scabbard the value is much enhanced. The general state of the bayonet and scabbard should be carefully examined for wear and condition but bear in mind that an old model bayonet in good or unused condition may well be a reproduction or unissued item—this is especially true of some German examples and in either case the decreased value should be reflected in the price. The actual model and type of bayonet may take some investigation and research and once more a simple model of bayonet can lead to absorbing and rewarding findings. To help in these investigations there are several very good books on the market and also some that are less easy to find as they have long been out of print.

A word of warning regarding edged weapons from Germany. The Nazi State produced a vast array of edged weapons ranging from dress daggers to hunting knives and small swords. Most were meant for dress purposes only and as a result many were ornate, covered in various NSDAP regalia and swastikas, and with their blades engraved or chased with party slogans. After 1945 thousands of these souvenirs of the NSDAP period in power were bought home by the conquering armies and ever since then they have been bought and sold on the open market. But being such intrinsically attractive items they have always attracted high prices and of late demand has been far outstripping supply. The result is that there are now huge numbers of reproduction Nazi daggers and knives on the market and if you are after an authentic example the motto to adopt must be 'let the buyer beware'. The truth is that, as with badges and regalia, the reproduction of Nazi daggers and knives has now become a minor industry. When the products of this 'industry' are advertised as such there is no harm done but all too often edged weapons are sold as authentic. Very often their attraction is enhanced by elaborate presentation in lined boxes or caskets which should warn the unwary but such is their attraction such obvious blandishments are often overlooked. The only course to adopt to avoid such reproductions is carefully to research the subject beforehand and buy only from reputable dealers. By doing this you might have to pay more than you expected but at least you won't be landed with a fake.

Chapter 13

Presentation of results

Research and delving into the recent military past can produce some surprising and rewarding results. Nearly anyone who has had a hand in any form of military archaeology has, at some time or another, produced something that is satisfying and well worth all the time and effort lavished, but all too often the finished (if research or renovation can ever be called finished) result seems to lack something. This 'something' is the need to share with an audience the pleasure and satisfaction which comes from a job well done. The renovation faction at least have a tangible end result in the shape of a well-turned out vehicle or restored structure for all to marvel at. The true archaeologist usually has a nice heap or array of military relics rescued from the soil, and the tape recorder has a rack of preserved prose to listen to and use. The collector can show off his bayonets, books or badges to anyone who can be persuaded to peruse them.

But for the pure researcher or historian, this is not always possible. What they have to show is usually a fat file of paper, and in many instances not even that, for the results are locked inside a memory bank in the human brain. For some individuals this is all they require from their activities, but in the past I have found such persons are few and far between. Most people yearn to share their knowledge with like-minded enthusiasts but all too often the question is, how?

There are several answers to this, and one of the most obvious solutions is to join an appropriate club or society. Depending on your interests, some form of body can be found which caters for your particular activity and several examples are scattered among the pages of this book. The problem is when you find yourself becoming involved in a certain field in which it appears no one else is interested, even if there are several peripheral areas. On the technical side of military equipment there seem to be large numbers of people involved in researching AFVs and their various aspects, but I have discovered that few seem to want to specialise in artillery alone. As a result I have been able to make personal contacts only by dint of sending numerous letters and having odd conversations in many quarters. This personal contact with like-minded souls is one of the more pleasant rewards of any social activity but personal conversations or letters are not the most lasting mediums in which to hand down permanent and meaningful research results. For the fact remains that to give your personal work some meaning it has to be shared by as many people as possible and not just a small circle for a short length of time. In order to make your efforts really worthwhile they have to be put on a more permanent footing. Perhaps the most common and lasting method of doing this is to put words on to paper by writing some form of report, article or book.

As soon as the word writing is mentioned to many people, a form of mental stop-page seems to afflict their thinking processes and they straight away come out with something along the lines of 'Oh, but I'm no good at writing anything, so I won't try.' This is a very understandable reaction but it does mean that your results will never reach a proper audience. Almost every aspect of military archaeology needs an end result and this always means some form of written word. If you are unwilling to put pen to paper you will be missing one of the more rewarding aspects of the activity. Another argument is that if you have been able to turn up something that is of value you have a virtual duty to let as many people as possible know about it. Otherwise your work will be duplicated by others at a great waste of effort and facilities, and there is also the historical aspect. What may seem like a trivial piece of work that is not worth recording today may well turn out to be tomorrow's priceless gem. Time and time again in these pages we have come across instances where this has been shown to be the case.

Having placed this section in its context, I will explain how this recording of valuable research results can be put on to the all-important paper. The methods mentioned will deal mainly with the pure research aspect but it will apply to just about every aspect of military archaeology dealt with in this book. Even the vehicle, weapon and badge buffs will discover that they, too, have writing to do and they would do well to avoid some of the pitfalls I will mention.

One of the first things to remember when you are about to start writing is that what you are doing is meant to last, and last not for just a few days or weeks but many years, especially if it is a report which will be filed. It has got to last physically as well as factually, and that means using decent quality materials. Make sure the paper you use is good robust stuff and not the dreadful flimsy muck so favoured by civil services as an economy measure. Binders need to be something a bit more substantial than thin cardboard or manilla folders—they are fine for general filing but not strong or durable enough for your finished work.

As a general rule any report, article or book manuscript will have to be typed. If you can't type you have two options. Either learn yourself, or get someone to type it for you. The latter may be very expensive if you get it done commercially, but not even my wife can read my handwriting so I used the former option and went to local evening classes to obtain the rudiments. Even now my typing is still not up to commercial standards but I can get by with the aid of correcting fluid and the like.

Having got the materials out of the way we can get on to the actual writing. Let us first consider the compilation of a final report on some finished programme. Even if you are likely to be the only reader it should still be carried out correctly. (Try to think along the lines that it is all good practice for the future.) Of course, one of the very first things to be sure about is that you have got all your facts right. This may sound so obvious that it does not warrant mention but all too often the opposite is true.

It is sometimes difficult to know exactly when a research programme has been properly concluded. Therefore, it is important to have a clear objective to begin with, for without one you will not have anything to assess your results by and you will have no idea of when the completion stage has been reached. As for the accuracy of your work, that is sometimes open to more than one opinion. Many people have written things which even a little work or reflection have shown to be incorrect, and wrong to the extent that their results have misled others as they have not been critically questioned. Try to study your own work objectively—if you are not sure of something, say so in your results. Some may not like this practice of turning out incomplete or partially correct work but I am of the school that would rather see something unfinished than waiting for the perfect work which may never be completed. Your efforts may persuade others to delve deeper and come up with the missing facts. But by saying this I am not trying to make excuses for poor or incomplete work, so the main objective must be to get it all as accurate as is humanly possible. This will mean getting second opinions, taking time to check and re-check everything and even going back to square one to go over all your findings yet again. One factor I have always found most useful when checking over a final draft is time. The space of only a few weeks will often be sufficient to clear your mind in order to enable a fresh look at your results which will help you reach an objective conclusion. Having established as far as possible that your work is complete and correct, the real task of writing can commence. This is the bit where you just have to start typing or writing your text on paper. But before you do that you should try to put all the main headings on to a separate sheet of paper and think about the sequence. Sequence is just the order in which you will be setting out your work. Ideally it should follow a nice easy-to-read path with everything in a logical order, but even a little practice will make this operation a relatively simple one.

For a formal end-of-project report an explanatory title is necessary but it need not be at the head of the first sheet—I find a separate leader sheet is best for that purpose and it can also be used for the names of the author(s), dates and so forth. A formal report should be prefaced with a short résumé paragraph giving a broad outline of what the report contains but this should be very brief (but comprehensive). Then follows the main meat of the work with everything laid out in logically sequenced paragraphs. Any illustrations should be kept on separate sheets, be they drawings or photographs, with annotations in the text. All such reports should be typed double-spaced on to sheets of paper of standard office sizes (this will assist in photocopying at a later date).

So far I have been writing this section as though an individual has been concerned and no one else. Very often writing a final report will be a group venture but in such instances a particular individual will have to be given an overall responsibility for producing the final document, otherwise the effect of many hands at the tiller will often result in a scrappy and disjointed report. The choice of person may be a tricky one but I am a firm believer that in such circumstances the decision must be seen to be a group one or otherwise feelings will be ruffled among the rest of the group.

Once completed the next problem comes with what to do with your carefully compiled report. All too often a useful piece of work is simply placed on the researcher's bookshelf and left there, and we are back to the 'lack of satisfaction syndrome' I mentioned earlier. The truth is that there are several outlets for your work. For a start copies could be sent to anyone who has assisted in the project. In my experience, very few researchers can compile a useful report without getting assistance or guidance from other individuals or museums/libraries and a copy should be sent to them—at the very least this is a social courtesy. By copies I mean photocopies, for carbon copies, after the first or top copy, usually deteriorate very quickly in quality and become illegible, while a decent photocopy will be as good as your original. Apart from those directly involved try to send copies to the local authority or museum concerned. They will usually be only too glad to be able to add something to their local archives and as the report will be carefuly annotated and filed you will have the reassurance that your work will still be available for many years to come for future generations to use.

Situations will arise when individuals or groups will think their findings are worthy of a wider audience and this is where we start to think in terms of articles or even books. Most writers in our specialised field usually start their writing careers with specialist magazines dealing with their particular subject, but I have yet to meet anyone who has been born with the ability to write commercial articles without a great deal of practice on report-writing or small contributions to specialist magazines. The specialist journals are a really good feature of the military archaeology scene as not only do they give a chance for researchers to spread their message, but they also provide a sympathetic platform for the embryo author to learn the craft of writing for an audience. Nearly every organisation mentioned in these pages issues a form of magazine or newsletter and these will usually provide an ideal outlet for your particular results. If you are looking for financial reward from such magazines you can forget about it, for there won't be any. But ask anyone who has contributed to these journals how they felt when their first words appeared in print and they will tell you that the reward was something that could not be measured in monetary terms.

When sending anything to these magazines bear in mind that your presentation will be as important as your content. Specialist magazine editors are usually hard-pressed individuals with very little spare time and if you can present your work in an easy-to-use form it has a far better chance of seeing circulation than a scruffy, badly typed manuscript.

Once away from the specialist magazine field we pass on to the commercial magazine scene. Here many researchers and historians will often find a ready market for their findings, but only if the work is good. Commercial magazine editors have a constant problem in finding enough quality articles to fill their pages and thus very often getting a feature published will be easier than you think. But this doesn't mean that just because you think you are sending off something good that it will automatically get published—it won't. The maxim to use is that if an editor thinks it is bad, it *is* bad, and his word is final. So don't be discouraged if your work is sent back the first few times. Get to know *why* it isn't good enough and adapt yourself to the editor's way of thinking. Every magazine has its own style and methods of presentation and the best way to know what is wanted is to read back numbers of the journal concerned and present your work in the same manner. Again, your presentation will be important, so follow my earlier advice on manuscript preparation and remember that some magazines may ask for an extra copy as well.

From magazines the next way of reaching a wide audience is through books. If you can afford to finance all the work involved you can publish your work privately and hope the market will respond and your outlay of thousands of pounds will be recouped. Very few of us can follow that path but it has been done. In my library I have two works that were published privately. One that has been mentioned elsewhere in these pages is Colin Partridge's *Hitler's Atlantic Wall* and there the quality of the book is so good that his investment will be recovered. Another excellent example of quality work getting its just desserts is a volume on the French Resistance, *Armement Clandestin* by Pierre Lorain, which is a really beautifully produced book and one well worth searching out. But as previously mentioned the costs alone will prevent all but the very largest and richest groups thinking in such terms, and the commercial publishing world will have to be involved.

Commercial publishers, like any other businesses, are in it for the money so if you approach them with a proposition they have got to think in terms of how much profit they are likely to gain from working with you. Such a specialised field as ours would seem unlikely to attract a wide audience and would thus seem to discourage the chance of anyone being able to get books published on their particular interests. However, the world of military archaeology is now expanding and becoming more and more of a viable proposition for publishers. Thus you may have a chance of seeing your work on the bookstalls.

But it will be no easy matter to persuade a commercial publisher that your work is worthy of consideration. Every week publishers receive hundreds of unsolicited manuscripts on all manner of topics but only a tiny minority ever get to the consideration stage. One factor which you will have to consider is whether or not the particular publishing house deals with your specialist field. Even a cursory browse in a bookshop will reveal that publishers tend to concentrate on particular subjects. Thus it would be no good you sending your manuscript on Medieaval Fortresses in Wolverhampton to a publishing house that deals mainly with crime thrillers—an extreme example but any publisher will tell you that it happens. Choose your publisher carefully and try to avoid subjects that are already on the market. No publisher wishes to produce books in opposition to others already available on the same topic.

What publishers require is a work which people will want to buy, that is well presented, and that is new. All too often publishers are offered texts that are mere rehashes of something that has been done before (and the same goes for magazines). They will usually only consider a duplication of something already on the market if it differs in some major way from what has gone before. If you have been following an original line of research you will have a far better chance of seeing your results in book form than if you are following a well-trodden path. The field of military archaeology is a very wide one, and one that is constantly expanding, so there should be room for everyone to make an original contribution, but instead publishers continue to be flooded with manuscripts on German tanks, the Atlantic Wall and the like.

Presentation to a publisher is just as important as it is to magazines, but as there is more finance at stake this presentation will need to be slightly different. If you feel you have something worth offering, *don't* send a publisher your complete manuscript straight out of the blue. What he will want to see is a brief outline of your work laid out on as small a number of sheets as possible. He will want to see what the book will cover, a provisional title, how many words will be involved, how many illustrations, any special features (such as a large number of plans or scale drawings) and a good reason why he should consider the submitted work at all. If this résumé tempts them you will be asked to submit a complete manuscript but this doesn't mean that it has been accepted for publication. It may well be sent back with a rejection slip, and the publisher is under no obligation to tell you why.

If the typescript is selected a contract will follow, and read this carefully as some considerable sums of money will be involved from that stage onwards. Of course, the publisher finances the production of the book and it is his responsibility to buy the paper, binding material, printing time, etc, but you will have to note carefully the manuscript or illustration delivery dates and, of course, you will be involved in the proof reading. Be very careful at this stage as you may find yourself having to alter some parts of your text on the actual proofs. If these alterations are substantial you may be liable for some of the costs involved—exactly how much will depend on the terms of your contract so read it carefully.

I have no wish to scare away any potential authors but the publishing world is a particularly hazardous one, even if it is most rewarding in financial terms and general esteem. Think carefully before you enter it—you may well be in for a long period of disappointments, frustrations and hard work. But eventually, if your work is good, your presentation up to the mark, and most important, you have a good slice of luck, you will have the deep satisfaction of seeing your books on the open market. Don't expect to make large sums of money as very few authors in our field can earn a living from writing. But it does produce its own particular rewards—try it and you will see what they are.

Appendix A

Channel Islands artillery

The article printed below has been chosen for inclusion primarily because it is an excellent example of a worth-while piece of research. The writer is Michael Ginns who lives in Jersey and was thus well placed to uncover the mass of material featured. Michael was inspired to put pen to paper when he discoverd that he had amassed a great deal of information as the result of protracted investigations into the units and weapons situated in the Channel Islands from 1940 to 1945. His research had shown that there was no listing of the artillery units used by the Germans, so he set about filling that gap.

Born British and bred a Jerseyman, Michael Ginns lived through the German Occupation and was, for a time, interned in South Germany, even though he was only 14 years old at the time. When the war was over Michael devoted his energies to railways and trams along with other public transport subjects, but gradually the Occupation years came to interest him more and he is now a leading light of the CIOS and his files cover almost every aspect of the Occupation.

The article was first published in an abridged form in the Channel Islands Occupation Review for 1975. The research for the text took several years and was carried out using numerous sources which are, correctly, acknowledged, and the author is pleased to mention that he was able to assist in a very small way as well. The reader will note that, although German artillery is the heart of the subject matter, many other avenues have been explored to provide a background for the study.

German Artillery in the Channel Islands

by Michael Ginns

It is by now a well-established fact that the Channel Islands were more heavily fortified than any other sector of Hitler's Atlantic Wall and, for their size, had a greater concentration of emplaced artillery than anywhere else in Western Europe. By the end of 1944, no fewer than 146 artillery weapons in 37 battery sites stood waiting for an enemy that never came. This figure does not take into account a further 107 coastal defence guns. It is necessary to emphasise at the outset that a coastal defence or anti-invasion gun, usually manned by infantry and with its own stretch of beach to defend, cannot count as coastal artillery which must be linked to a fire control centre to enable the guns to fire out to sea. The distinction becomes further blurred when identical weapons are found acting in both capacities.

Without further preamble it can be stated that German artillery in the Channel Islands fell into two categories—coastal and divisional. With coastal artillery there were two agencies involved, namely the Navy and the Army. The task of the coastal artillery was threefold: a) To protect German shipping passing between the Islands themselves and the adjacent French coast, as well as naval vessels passing along the so-called 'core' route between Cherbourg and Brest; b) To protect the entire Gulf of St Malo against invasion; and c) To prevent landings in the Islands themselves.

In this latter task the coastal batteries were to be assisted by the divisional batteries of Artillerie Regiment 319.

Overall command

Throughout Western Europe the overall command of batteries firing at sea targets was in the hands of the German Navy. This was the direct result of Hitler's Directive No 41, issued on March 23 1942 and compiled at the request of officials of the German High Command (OKW) to sort out an existing confused command situation which had caused many arguments. During the preparation of the Directive (according to Warlimont's *Inside Hitler's HQ*) the Naval C-in-C added to and twisted the wording to give superior power to the Navy over command of the coastal batteries in the event of an invasion. In effect this meant the Navy was in charge, but only as long as the approaching enemy was *on the sea*. As soon as the enemy came ashore then, and only then, could the local Army commander take over.

To the dismay of the Army High Command (OKH), Hitler accepted and approved these proposals without question. Thus an already confused command structure was made worse. When would the Army take over? When the enemy was actually on the beach? Ten metres off-shore? Or as troops were leaping into the surf? With the petty jealousies and power-seeking among the sycophants at OKW added to the bitter inter-service rivalries, the Directive's orders were doomed to failure from the outset. No one benefited except Hitler who liked to keep all the reins of power in his own hands.

It was not long before the two services were sniping at each other. The Army accused the Navy of siting its batteries irresponsibly by placing them in exposed positions on headlands which they treated like the foredeck of a battleship. The Navy did this as they were used to having their guns mounted on a ship and being able actually to see their targets. The Navy, in their turn, accused the Army batteries of skulking inland out of sight of the sea.

Naval Command in the Channel Islands

Prior to 1942 the German Navy in Channel Islands waters came under the jurisdiction of Seeko-Cherbourg (Seeko—Kommandeur der Seeverteidigung—Commander of Sea Defences, or Naval Commander), but in that year the Channel Islands became a Naval Command in their own right under the Seeko-KI (KI—Kanalinseln—Channel Islands), who, after occupying a temporary headquarters for some time, moved into a very substantial bunker at St Jaques, Guernsey, in February 1944. It was to Seeko-KI that the artillery commanders in the Islands had to refer when requesting permission to open fire.

Having set the scene, I now propose to examine in detail the various agencies that provided artillery cover in the Islands and the batteries under their command.

a) Navy coastal batteries

The coastal batteries of the Navy in the Islands came under the jurisdiction of two MAA (Marine Artillerie Abteilung—Navy Artillery Battalion). The first to arrive was:

Marine Artillerie Abteilung 604
Headquarters: St Martin, Guernsey
This unit, which had seen service in Holland, first came to the Channel Islands in

March 1941 and controlled the following batteries:

Batterie Strassburg. Jerbourg Point, Guernsey. Four 22 cm K 532(f). This battery was intended for conversion to 15 cm SK C/28 guns but this was never implemented.

Batterie Lotheringen. Noirmont Point, Jersey. Four 15 cm SK L/45. Intended for conversion to 15 cm SK C/28 guns—not implemented. Also used two 7.5 cm FK 231(f) field guns as Nahkampfkanonen (close combat guns).

Batterie Elsass. Fort Albert, Alderney. Three 17 cm SK L/40. This battery, together with later Navy batteries on Alderney, was handed over to MAA 605 in June 1942.

Batterie Steinbruch. Les Vardes, Guernsey. Four 15 cm SK C/28. This battery did not become operational until after October 1942 and was one of the few built to strict fortress standards from scratch (ie, with turret guns mounted in emplacements with concrete at least two metres thick). During construction the area was covered by an Army battery in temporary emplacements. Two 7.5 cm FK 231(f) were also mounted.

Batterie Mirus. La Frie Baton, Guernsey. Four 30.5 cm K(E)626(r). This was the largest battery in the Channel Islands. When Hitler ordered that the Islands be converted into fortresses, he also stipulated that 38 cm batteries be placed on Guernsey, at Jobourg on the Cotentin Peninsula, and on the north coast of Brittany, thus sealing the Gulf of St Malo. The 38 cm guns were unavailable and 20.3 cm railway guns were installed on the French coast. The Jobourg guns, together with those of Batterie Mirus, effectively sealed the northern approaches to the Gulf, but to the south there was a gap in the defences. Neither the Britanny guns, nor the Mirus ones could reach the 50 km range needed, and indeed Mirus had to struggle to attain the 42 km necessary to reach the west coast of Jersey. None the less, Mirus was a daunting prospect. The construction of the site took 18 months, consumed 47,000 metres of concrete, and seriously delayed many other projects. As well as the huge gun emplacements, there were crew quarters, a hospital (all centrally heated), a small arms store, huge ammunition bunkers, close combat and AA guns, a water storage system, and radar and fire control centres. The complex sprawled over many acres and was manned by a crew of 480. The first gun fired its trial shot on April 13 1942 and by August 12 the guns were operational, although they were not officially handed over to the Navy by Krupps (who supervised the installations) until November 1942. The battery was named after Kapitan zur See Mirus, a naval artillery expert, who was killed in an attack by British aircraft on the ship on which he was travelling between Alderney and Guernsey.

Batterie Klein Sark. Little Sark. Three 8.8 cm SK. For most of the war Sark was not heavily defended, being garrisoned by a reinforced company of Infantrie Regiment 584. This unit was issued with two mobile (as opposed to the more usual casemated) 10.5 cm K 331(f) guns acting in a coast defence role. Until late 1944 these were the only artillery pieces on Sark but on July 27 of that year a small German naval vessel, the VP 203 (VP—Vorposten—outpost boat) was sunk in St Peter Port Harbour in a rocket attack by a British fighter-bomber. The guns were subsequently salvaged, taken to Sark and mounted on Little Sark to form Batterie Klein Sark. Whether there was any tactical advantage or necessity for this battery is doubtful. More likely than not it was constructed to give work to hands that would otherwise have been idle due to the laying up of many German vessels in Channel Island harbours when ports in France fell to the Allies.

Marine Artillerie Abteilung 605

Headquarters: Fort Albert, Alderney (June 1942 to sometime in 1943). Bunker near St Anne, Alderney (sometime in 1943 onwards).

As Batterie Mirus became operational it absorbed the energies of MAA 604 to such effect that a new battalion, MAA 605, moved into Alderney on or about June 20 1942 to take over the naval batteries there. The CO was also Arko (Artillerie Kommandeur—Artillery Commander) for Alderney. MAA 605 controlled the following batteries:

Batterie Elsass. Fort Albert, Alderney. Three 17 cm SK L/40. Intended for conversion to 15 cm SK C/28 guns but never implemented. Also mounted two 7.5 cm FK 231(f).

Batterie Annes. La Giffoire, Alderney. Two 15 cm K 18 (August 1942 to January 1943). Four 15 cm SK C/28 (January 1943 onwards). While under construction the area eventually covered by Annes was protected by two Army guns (12/HKAR 1265) and the site was then known as Batterie West or the Weststellung.

Batterie General der Artillerie Marcks. West slopes of Fort Albert, Alderney. Four 10.5 cm K 331(f). This was the Alderney harbour blocking battery and had a restricted field of fire, the guns being mounted in fortress-type casemates let into the hillside. The battery was a late starter, completed not earlier than April 1944. It is believed to have been originally named Rosenfest and was renamed Marcks in honour of the General who commanded LXXXIV Corps (in whose area the Islands lay) and who was killed on June 12 1944.

b) Army coastal batteries

The first Army coastal batteries arrived in the Channel Islands at the same time as those of the Navy. Four batteries were in transit during March 1941—two to Guernsey and two to Jersey.

By mid-1941 the decision had been taken to increase the Channel Island defences and on June 13 movement orders went out to numbers of HKB (Heeres Küsten Batterie—Army Coastal Battery) to assemble in Granville and St Malo for transportation to the Islands. Only one battery (HKB 461) proceeded via Granville en route to Alderney—that was on July 15 1941. By July 26, HKB 462 was reported to be in Germany and on the same date seven other batteries (463-469) were in St Malo in various stages of readiness. Some had guns and crews but no ammunition while others had guns and ammunition but no crews. Three other units (470-472) were also assembling in the XVI Army area and they had crews and ammunition but no guns!

It should be noted that during this period this collection of batteries, armed with a variety of German and captured equipment, did not form part of any regiment but were individual units known as Corps or GHQ units, these being at the disposal of Corps or Army commanders for attachment to divisions for special purposes.

It would also be relevant to point out that it was the OKW intention to convert the Channel Islands into *naval* fortresses and that ultimately all the principal batteries would be manned by the Navy and, with the exception of Mirus, armed with modern 15 cm SK C/28 guns in turrets. Indeed, in July 1941, German records indicate that the concentration of batteries in the Channel Islands had used up all the medium battery reserves in the west. Thus OKH were at pains to request that the Navy should take over the responsibility for manning the batteries and added that it was not an Army responsibility to fire at sea targets.

Eight batteries were to have been equipped with 15 cm SK C/28 guns—three in Jersey and two each in Guernsey and Alderney. Only two were so armed and before more conversions were made an Allied air raid disrupted the German production lines. One consequence of this, as far as the Channel Islands were concerned, was that in 1943 the individual Army batteries were re-constituted as HKAR 1265 (Heeres Küsten Artillerie Regiment—Army Coastal Artillery Regiment).

Typical 15 cm sFH 18 installation. As a general rule Army batteries were far less elaborate than Navy installations in the Channel Islands, and Army guns were often temporarily emplaced to 'cover' construction work on the larger and more static batteries.

The framework on which to build the regiment already existed. The batteries were arranged in four groups, two to each of the larger islands and each controlled by an HKAA (Heeres Küsten Artillerie Abteiling—Army Coastal Artillery Battalion). These were in turn controlled by the staff of Artillerie Regiment 720 zbV (zu besondere Verwendung—for special employment). This became the new Regimental HQ of HKAR 1265, the deployment of which, and the subordinate battalion, was as follows:

Heeres Küsten Artillerie Regiment 1265
Headquarters: 'Tannenberg', Oberlands Road, St Martin, Guernsey. The CO was also Arko, Guernsey.

First Battalion (I/HKAR 1265—formerly HKAA 440)
Headquarters: Near Mont Rossignol, Jersey (August 1941 to September 1944). Mont Orgueil Castle, Jersey (September 1944 onwards).

I/HKAR 1265 was originally a medium howitzer battalion but in August 1944 two medium field gun batteries were moved from Guernsey to Jersey and attached to the First Battalion. This was after the fall of Normandy to the Allies when it was expected that Jersey would be attacked from the east. The CO of I/HKAR 1265 then

Above *The massive sliding breech of a 15 cm sFH 18.* **Below** *Numerous 27 cm Mrs 18 batteries were emplaced in the Channel Islands. It is not certain that this piece was actually one of those emplaced in the Islands but it is typical of many of the installations there. This example is emplaced in a typical circular pit with ammunition and firing platform fittings. In the background work is still in progress on building the battery installations and a concrete mixer can be seen along with camouflage netting and what appears to be a stone crusher.*

became the Commander of Seezielbekämpfungsgruppe Ost (Sea Targets Battle Group East) which was formed to counter any such eventuality. Batteries included in I/HKAR were:

Batterie Hindenburg (formerly Batterie Red Houses). North of Route Orange, St Brelade, Jersey. Unit: 1/HKAR 1265 (formerly HKB 467). Three 21 cm Mrs 18.

Batterie Ludendorff (formerly Batterie St Ouens). Rue du Douet, St Ouens, Jersey (August 1941 to some time in 1942. La Chasse de l'Eglise, St Ouens, from then onwards). Unit: 2/HKAR 1265 (formerly HKB 469). Three 21 cm Mrs 18.

Batterie Mackensen (formerly Batterie St Martin). Rue de la Fosse à Gres, St Martin, Jersey (August 1942 onwards). Unit: 3/HKAR 1265 (formerly HKB 469). Three 21 cm Mrs 18.

Second Battalion (II/HKAR 1265—formerly HKAA 728)
Headquarters: Mont au Roux, St Brelade, Jersey (July 1941 to some time in 1942, Old Semaphore Station, La Moye, from then onwards).

Batteries included in II/HKAR 1265 were:

Batterie Endrass. Mont Rossignol, St Ouens, Jersey (2 guns) and St Helier, Jersey (2 guns), (March 1941 to June 1942). Westmount (June 1942 onwards). Unit: 4/HKAR 1265 (formerly HKB 355). Four 7.5 cm FK 231(f) (March 1941 to June 1942). Four 10.5 cm K 311(f) (June 1942 onwards). This was one of the batteries which arrived in March 1941. In 1942 the 7.5 cm guns were passed to the infantry for coastal defence and 10.5 cm guns taken over for use as the harbour blocking battery.

Batterie Moltke (formerly Batterie Les Landes). Les Landes, St Ouens, Jersey. Unit: 5/HKAR 1265 (formerly HKB 356). Four 15.5 cm K 418(f). Intended for conversion to 15 cm SK C/28 and the turrets arrived in Jersey in June 1943. After lying around for almost a year they were taken back to France.

Batterie Roon (formerly Batterie La Moye). La Moye Point, St Brelade, Jersey. Unit: 6/HKAR (formerly HKB 470). Four 22 cm K 532(f). The position was ready by September 9 1941 but the guns were not emplaced before December 12 1941. On August 19 1944 one gun was destroyed by the premature detonation of a shell in the breech.

Third Battalion (III/HKAR 1265—formerly HKAA 452)
Headquarters: Ruette de l'Eglise, Catel, Guernsey.

Arrived in December 1941. Batteries were:

Batterie Elefant (formerly Batterie Chaumiere). La Chaumiere, Catel, Guernsey. Unit: 7/HKAR 1265 (formerly HKB 464). Three 21 cm Mrs 18.

Batterie Mammuth (formerly Batterie Effards). Les Effards, Catel, Guernsey. Unit: 8/HKAR 1265 (formerly HKB 465). Three 21 cm Mrs 18.

Batterie Rhinozeros (formerly Batterie Beaucamps). Les Beaucamps, Catel, Guernsey. Unit: 9/HKAR 1265 (formerly HKB 466). Three 21 cm Mrs 18.

Fourth Battalion (IV/HKAR 1265—formerly HKAA 727)
Headquarters: St Peter's Arsenal, St Peter in the Wood, Guernsey.

HKAA 727 arrived in July 1941. Subordinate batteries were:

Batterie Barbara. North View, Guernsey. Unit: 10/HKAR 1265 (formerly HKB 354). Four 15.5 cm K 418(f). St Barbara is the patron saint of gunners.

Batterie Naumannshöhe. Les Sages, St Peter, Guernsey (2 guns) and Fort George, Guernsey (2 guns) from March 1941 until some time in 1942. St Peter Port, Guernsey, from then onwards. Unit: 11/HKAR 1265 (formerly HKB 353). Four 7.5 cm FK 231(f) from March 1941 until some time in 1942. Four 10.5 cm K 331(f) from then onwards. This was one of the first batteries to arrive in Guernsey in March

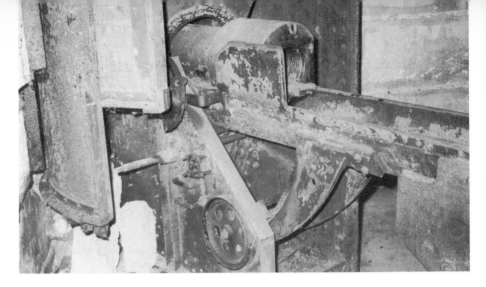

As we closed for press I had the opportunity to see inside a beach defence bunker at La Corbiere, Jersey. This bunker has been buried (deliberately) since 1948 and is thus still very much as it was prior to the end of the war in 1945. The bunker has been handed over to the care of the CIOS who plan to renovate the structure and restore it as nearly as possible to its original state. The bunker is unusual in that it still retains its main armament, a 10.5 cm K 331(f). Numbers of this French gun were captured by the Germans in 1940 and removed from their field carriages for mounting as beach defence guns along the Atlantic Wall (French designation was Canon de 105 mle 1913 Schneider). Although this example lacks its breech block (and a few other bits and pieces) the CIOS have already got hold of another. Even as seen here the La Corbiere bunker is a really unique example of a piece of living history that can still be touched and sampled, and the CIOS are to be once more congratulated on their enterprise.

1941 and was emplaced in two platoons. During 1942 it was converted to a harbour blocking battery.

Batterie Blücher (formerly Batterie Ost or Oststellung). St Anne, Alderney. Unit: 12/HKAR 1265 (formerly HKB 461—see below). Two 15 cm K 18 (July 1941 to January 1943). Four 15 cm K 18 (January 1943 onwards). Records show that HKB 461 arrived in Alderney in 1941 but by 1942 it had been replaced by HKB 462—doubtless only the unit was transferred, the guns staying where they were. At first these guns were installed in two platoons with two guns in the Weststellung and two in the Oststellung. When Annes became operational the two platoons combined and the site was renamed Blücher. After D-Day in 1944 it was this battery that harassed troop concentrations on the Contenin and caused Alderney to be shelled by the 16-inch guns of HMS *Rodney*. Despite a two-hour bombardment, casualties were light and only one gun was damaged (and later repaired).

Batterie Gneisenau (formerly Batterie Cobo). Les Vardes, St Sampson, Guernsey (August 1941 to May 1942. Then Cobo, Catel, Guernsey from October 1942 to August 1944). Unit: 13/HKAR 1265 (formerly HKB 462—see below). Four 15 cm K 18. While at Les Vardes this battery used the Batterie Steinbruch area. The battery was later manned by HKB 461 from Alderney, but the true picture is now difficult to establish—see below. In August 1944, 13/HKAR 1265 moved to Jersey with its guns and formed into Batterie Schlieffen attached to I/HKAR 1265.

Batterie Scharnhorst (formerly Batterie Arsenal). Les Islets Arsenal, St Saviour, Guernsey. Unit: 14/HKAR 1265 (formerly HKB 463—see below). Four 15 cm K 18 (August 1941 to August 1944). As the most detailed records of battery positions date from after August 1944, ie, after 13/ and 14/HKAR 1265 had moved to Jersey, it is difficult to be precise as to which unit manned which 15 cm K 18 battery in the first three years, as the three units (HKB 461, 462 and 463) rotated in turn to man Blücher on Alderney.

Batterie Generaloberst Dollman (formerly Batterie Pleinmont). Pleinmont, Torteval, Guernsey. Unit: 15/HKAR 1265 (formerly HKB 471). Four 22 cm K 532(f). The emplacements were ready by September 1941 but the guns did not arrive until December. This battery was intended for conversion to 15 cm SK C/28 guns but this was never implemented. Named after Generaloberst Dollman who commanded the VII Army, of which the 319 Infantry Division (the division based in the Islands) was part from June 1942 until August 1944.

Batterie Radetzky (formerly Batterie l'Eree). St Peter, Guernsey. Unit: 16/HKAR 1265 (formerly HKB 472). Four 22 cm K 532(f). Situated almost under the muzzles of Mirus. It was intended to transfer the battery and guns to Alderney in late 1942 but the move was never made.

c) **Army divisional batteries**

It was common practice (although by no means mandatory) for supporting units in German divisions to bear the same number as the parent unit. Thus the artillery regiment with the 319 Infantry Division was AR 319 (AR—artillery regiment). It should also be noted that, in accordance with Hitler's Directive that the 319 Division be reinforced over and above the strength of a normal division, AR 319 carried four, rather than the normal three, battalions on its strength. Unlike their coastal brethren, and although they were installed in prepared positions, the divisional batteries were fully mobile (motor or horse-drawn) and could be moved about their respective island as required. At several points alternative positions had been prepared ready to receive them with communications, etc, already laid on.

Artillerie Regiment 319
Headquarters: Kernwerk (Battle HQ), l'Aleval, St Peter, Jersey. Alternative HQ at
Beaumont. The CO was Arko, Jersey.

First Battalion (I/AP 319).
Headquarters: 'Greygables', La Haule, St Brelade, Jersey (November 1941 to some
time in 1943. Then moved to a command bunker near Mont de la Roque Hotel, also
at St Brelade).
Batterie Derrflinger. Belle Vue, Mont de la Roque, Jersey. Units: 1/AR 319
(December 1941 to June 1944). Kanonenzug Aubin (June 1944 onwards). Four 8 cm
FK 30(t), (December 1941 to June 1944). Two 8 cm FK 30(t) (June 1944 onwards).
With the shift in the defences to the east of Jersey in mid-1944, this battery lost two of
its guns and was reduced to a Kanonenzug (gun platoon) manned by troops from the
nearby Battalion HQ.
Batterie Seydlitz. Mont au Roux, St Brelade, Jersey. Unit: 2/AR 319. Four 8 cm FK
30(t).
Batterie Ziethen. La Moye Hotel, St Brelade, Jersey (November 1941 to April 1943).
Point de l'Oeillere, St Brelade, Jersey (April 1943 onwards). Unit: 3/AR 319. Four
8 cm FK 30(t) (November 1941 to April 1943). Four 10 cm leFH 14/19(t) (April 1943
onwards). In order to bring AR 319 up to strength artillery units in France were
combed for men and guns. 3/AR 319 was originally part of Artillerie Abteilung 651
of the 711 Infantry Division (XV Army).

Second Battalion (II/AR 319).
Headquarters: Palace Hotel, St Saviour, Jersey (June 1941 to some time in 1942).
Nicolle Tower, St Clement, Jersey (1942-43). Mont Mallet, Gorey, Jersey (1943
onwards).
Batterie Seekt. Westmount, Jersey (June 1941 to June 1942). St Clement, Jersey
(June 1942 onwards). Unit: 4/AR 319. Four 10 cm leFH 14/19(t). This battery acted
as harbour blocking battery until Endrass was ready.
Batterie Fritsch. St Lawrence, Jersey. Unit: 5/AR 319 (June 1941 to June 1944).
1/AR 319 (June 1944 onwards). Four 10 cm leFH 14/19(t).
Batterie Dietl. Maufort Road, St Saviour, Jersey. Unit: 5/AR 319 (after June 1944).
Four 10 cm leFH 14/19(t).
Batterie Brauchitsch. Daisy Hill, Gorey, Jersey. Unit: 6/AR 319. Four 10 cm leFH
14/19(t). This unit was a reinforcement which came from AR 246 of the 246 Infantry
Division in November 1941.

Third Battalion (III/AR 319).
Headquarters: Les Vardes, St Peter Port, Guernsey.
    The battalion staff arrived in Guernsey on or about July 1 1941 and while in transit
were based for about six weeks in Jersey.
Batterie Georgefest. Fort George, St Peter Port, Guernsey. Unit: 9/AR 319
(November 1941 to some time in 1943). 7/AR 319 (1943 onwards). Four 10 cm leFH
14/19(t).
Batterie Sperber. Delancey Park, St Sampson, Guernsey. Unit: 7/AR 319 (June
1941 to some time in 1942). 8/AR 319 (1942 onwards). Sperber guarded the
approaches to St Peter Port Harbour and the guns were in casemates. 8/AR 319
spent about three weeks in Jersey in June 1941 while in transit to Guernsey.
Batterie Tiger. Best's Brickfields, St Andrew, Guernsey. Unit: 10/AR 319
(December 1941 to some time in 1943). 9/AR 319 (1943 onwards). Four 10 cm leFH

This piece is a 15 cm K 18, the same type of gun that was fired from Alderney towards the Cherbourg Peninsula during 1944 and 1945. The idea was to deliver general harrassing fire to the area and little damage was actually caused. But as a result the island of Alderney was bombarded by the 16-inch naval guns of HMS Rodney *but little damage resulted and there were few casualties. One 15 cm K 18 was damaged, however, as the recuperator was hit (the recuperator is the cylinder over the gun barrel) but it was soon repaired by replacing it with a modified gas cylinder.*

14/19(t). 9/AR 319 was a reinforcement coming from Artillerie Abteilung 715 of 715 Infantry Division (VI Army).

Fourth Battalion (IV/AR 319).
Headquarters: Les Eturs House, St Leonards, Guernsey.
   The entire Fourth Battalion was the reinforcing unit which gave AR 319 the 12 guns over and above the normal strength of a divisional AR. Formerly Artillerie Abteilung 652 of the 712 Infantry Division.
Batterie Wolf. Talbot Valley, Catel, Guernsey. Unit: 11/AR 319 (December 1941 to some time in 1943). 10/AR 319 (1943 onwards). Four 10 cm leFH 14/19(t).
Batterie Falke. South coast of Alderney. Units: 8/AR 319 (November 1941 to some time in 1942). 7/AR 319 (1942 to some time in 1943). 11/AR 319 (1943 onwards). Four 10 cm leFH 14/19(t).
Batterie Lux. Mont Saint, St Saviour, Guernsey. Unit: 12/AR 319. Four 10 cm leFH 14/19(t).

   As will be seen from the above, the situation in Guernsey was complicated as the units manning the batteries rotated in order to relieve the Alderney garrison—never a popular posting.

The weapons	Number in islands
30.5 cm K(E) 626(r). Maximum range 42,000 m	4
22 cm K 532(f). Range 21,800 m	12
21 cm Mrs 18. Range 18,600 m	18
17 cm SK L/40. Range 22,000 m	3
15.5 cm K 418(f). Range 18,600 m	8
15 cm SK L/45. Range 14,000 m	4
15 cm SK C/28. Range 22,000 m	8
15 cm K 18. Range 24,800 m	12
10.5 cm K 331(f). Range 8,200 m	12
10 cm leFH 14/19(t). Range 9,600 m	44
8.8 cm SK. Range unknown	3
8.76 cm FK 281(e). Range 11,000 m	7
8 cm FK 30(t). Range 13,300 m	6
7.5 cm FK 231(f). Range 11,100 m	8

To the above there must be added the further weapons that were used for purely coast defence purposes manned by the infantry, and the anti-aircraft guns of the Luftwaffe which could assist the other artillery in various roles.

10.5 cm K 331(f). Range 8,200 m	79
8 cm FK 30(t). Range 13,300 m	6
7.5 cm FK 231(f). Range 11,100 m	6
8.8 cm Flak 18, 36 or 37 anti-aircraft guns	96 (at least)

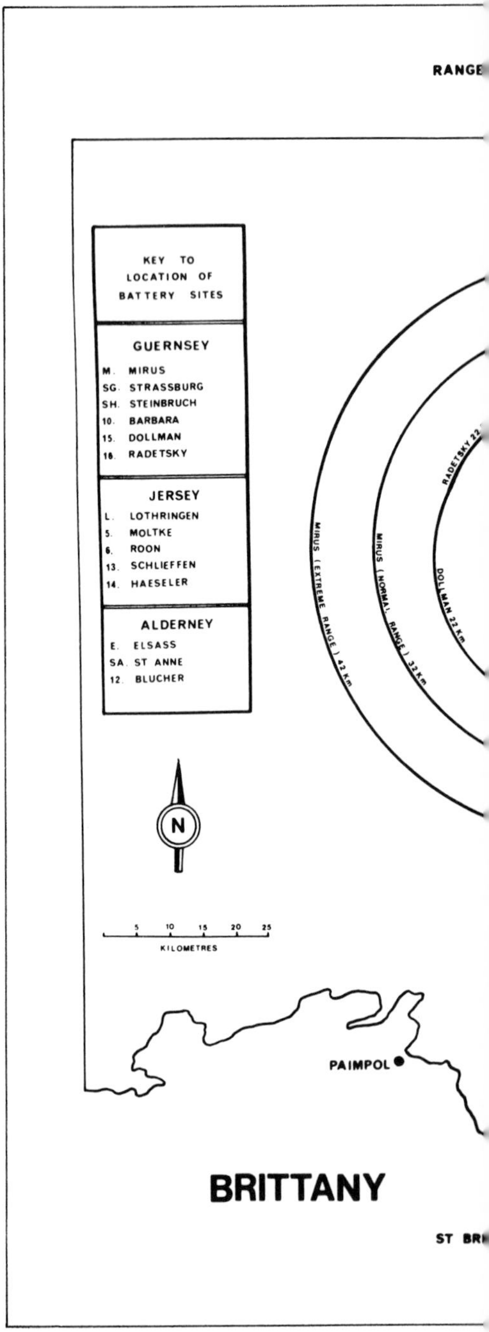

KEY TO LOCATION OF BATTERY SITES
GUERNSEY
M. MIRUS
SG. STRASSBURG
SH. STEINBRUCH
10. BARBARA
15. DOLLMAN
16. RADETSKY
JERSEY
L. LOTHRINGEN
5. MOLTKE
6. ROON
13. SCHLIEFFEN
14. HAESELER
ALDERNEY
E. ELSASS
SA. ST ANNE
12. BLUCHER
MIRUS (EXTREME RANGE) 42 Km
MIRUS (NORMAL RANGE) 32 Km
DOLLMAN 22 Km
N
5 10 15 20 25
KILOMETRES
PAIMPOL
BRITTANY

All round fire or overhead protection?

This subject was the cause of much argument at OKW. In May 1942 Hitler ordered that all gun sites on the coast of France were, if possible, to be provided with overhead protection. Artillery experts objected, and said that this would restrict the

L COASTAL ARTILLERY BATTERIES IN THE CHANNEL ISLANDS

EMPLACED FROM SEPTEMBER 1944 ONWARDS

(HOWITZER & HARBOUR BLOCKING BATTERIES ARE OMITTED)

S J SLOAN 74

gun's field of fire and make all-round defence impossible. Hitler retorted that an attack which achieved only limited success could damage the guns with splinters and so decimate the crews that firing would become impossible without overhead protection—all-round or otherwise!

A glance at the map will show that the principles of all-round fire were applied generally to the Channel Islands, save for those batteries (such as the harbour blocking ones) that had special tasks. This made sense, for the guns of the larger calibres—as well as firing at targets to their front—were equally capable of firing across country at targets well out to sea on the far side of the island on which the guns were emplaced. Indeed, during practice shoots they occasionally did this (much to the alarm of the inhabitants) and to aid this task a comprehensive system of observation posts was set up around the Islands.

The turret-mounted 15 cm SK C/28 combined the virtues of both requirements as it could traverse through 360° and the turret gave protection from all angles except the rear. It was for these reasons that it was chosen for general use in the Islands, although, in the event, only two batteries were so equipped.

Scrapped, or a watery grave

The curious will naturally be wondering if this concentration of artillery ever saw any action. Certainly the divisional batteries never fired a shot in anger. The coastal batteries were employed after June 1944 when they fired on Allied shipping that came too close, and on a few occasions they were able to inflict damage.

It has been said that the best contribution that the Channel Islands made to the Allied war effort was to be occupied. As a result of the Occupation, and Hitler's obsession with fortifying the Islands, men and materials were diverted from other fronts where they would have been far more gainfully employed. Certainly this was nowhere truer than in the case of the artillery. Had all, or indeed any, of the guns so uselessly emplaced on the Islands been available in France they may well have tipped the balance in favour of the Germans in several of the decisive battles in Normandy in June/July 1944.

After the war, when they had all been inspected by Allied experts, the guns awaited their fate. Despite an early and unsuccessful attempt by the States of Guernsey to preserve at least one gun and part of Batterie Mirus for posterity, all the big guns in Guernsey were cut up for scrap and exported. The smaller, mobile pieces were placed in one of the many tunnels excavated by the Germans and sealed in. A few years later, with scrap metal fetching enormous prices, they were exhumed and sold as scrap—nobody gave a thought to the preservation angle.

In Jersey the clearing up of German relics was carried out with even more haste and lack of thought for the future. All the big guns were removed from their carriages and dumped over the cliffs at Les Landes, St Ouen. The mobile guns were all taken out to sea and dumped. This should have been done in deep water, in the Hurd Deep off Alderney, but at least one cargo was disposed of off La Corbiere, Jersey, where they still lie waiting to trap the nets of unwary fishermen.

Acknowledgements and sources

The author wishes to thank the following for assistance so willingly given in the compilation of this article: R. Heaume and D. Kreckler of Guernsey; Ian Hogg and Terry Gander; and Denis Holmes for permission to consult his unique document *Auf die Kanalinseln*, this being the uncompleted memoirs of the late Vice-Admiral Hüffmeier. *Taktische Uberzeitung der Festungbereich Jersey* (in Societe Jersaise). *Artillerie Ausbau, Jersey* (Priaulx Library, Guernsey).
Microfilm Publications MoD 652, 653. MoD London (Naval Historical Branch).

Appendix B

List of ports and locations defended by coastal batteries between 1939 and 1945

The following list is based on a document dated March 16 1942 and covers all the various ports and coastal locations defended by coastal batteries. This list is included to give some idea of the locations worthy of investigation. Some of the sites, such as Dover, have already been the subject of a great deal of research, but many of the smaller ports mentioned will be well worth further investigation. At some of them there are still tangible remains, some are still occupied by various government bodies and many sites will have passed into private ownership. However, if you are in the locality of any of the sites mentioned below, they may form the basis for some interesting projects.

The sites listed were all coastal defence batteries but they were kept at various states of readiness and manning. Those mentioned first are the batteries manned full-time. Following them come batteries which were fully manned but were only intended for close defence of harbours. After that the battery importance is explained for each section. Every part starts in the north and ends up with batteries on the south coast. In each case the battery name is given first followed by the location—in many instances these are the same.

Full-time major batteries

Greenhead	Shetlands	North Denes	Yarmouth
Ness of Sound	Shetlands	Lowestoft	Lowestoft
Stromness	Orkneys	Landguard	Harwich
Stanger	Orkneys	Langdon	Dover
Rerwick	Orkneys	Newhaven Fort	Newhaven
Galtness 4.7 inch	Orkneys	Nodes 6 inch	Isle of Wight
South Sutor	Cromarty	Nomansland	Portsmouth
Torry Point	Aberdeen	Boulder	Isle of Wight
Salthouse	Peterhead	Breakwater	Portland
Broughty	Dundee	Drakes 6 inch	Plymouth
Kincraig	Forth	Picklecombe	Plymouth
Inchkieth North	Forth	Half Moon	Falmouth
Toward	Clyde	Nells Point	Barry
Loch Ewe	Loch Ewe	Mumbles Island	Swansea
Seaton	Blyth	West Blockhouse	Milford Haven
Castle 6 inch	Tyne	Soldiers Rock	Milford Haven
Roker	Sunderland	Crosby	Liverpool
South Gare	Tees	Holyhead	Holyhead
Spurn 6 inch	Humber	Fleetwood	Fleetwood
Links	Yarmouth	Workington	Workington

Part-time major batteries

Sullom Voe	Shetlands	Brownsea	Poole
Scalloway	Shetlands	Dartmouth 4.7 inch	Dartmouth
Wick	Wick	Brixham	Brixham
Montrose	Montrose	Fowey	Fowey
Finnart	Stranraer	Appledore 4.7 inch	Barnstaple
Ardhallow	Clyde	Hayle	Hayle
Bull Sand Fort 6 inch	Humber	Old Lighthouse	Port Talbot
Heugh	Hartlepool	Fishguard	Fishguard
Gibraltar Point	Skegness	Perch Rock	Liverpool
Spurn 4 inch	Humber	Lytham	Preston
Mersea East	Brightlingsea	Hilpsford	Barrow
Shoreham	Shoreham	Whitehaven	Whitehaven
Littlehampton	Littlehampton		

Close-defence batteries

Hoxa	Orkneys	Cliff End	Isle of Wight
Inchkeith South	Forth	Horse Sand	Portsmouth
Leith Docks	Forth	Spit Sand	Portsmouth
Cloch Point	Clyde	Nothe	Portland
Spanish	Tynemouth	Dartmouth 6 inch	Dartmouth
Grand	Lowestoft	Watchhouse	Plymouth
Beacon Hill	Harwich	St Anthonys	Falmouth
Grain	Thames and Medway	Roselands	Falmouth
Garrison Point	Thames and Medway	Lavernock Point	Severn Defences
Canvey	Thames and Medway	Flatholm North and South	Severn Defences
South Breakwater	Dover	Steepholme North and South	Severn Defences
Pier Turret	Dover	Brean Down	Severn Defences
Knuckle	Dover	Mumbles Hill	Swansea

Part-time close-defence batteries

Wellington	Orkneys	Kinsgate	Broadstairs
Nigg	Invergordon	Dumpton Point	Broadstairs
Fort George	Inverness	Ramsgate	Ramsgate
Innes Links	Lossiemouth	Bethlehem	Pegwell Bay
Girdleness	Aberdeen	Sandwich Bay	Sandwich Bay
Stannergate	Dundee	Sandown Castle	Deal
Inchkeith West	Forth	Deal	Deal
Pettycur	Forth	Kingsdown	Walmer
Fidra	Berwick	Western Heights	Dover
Amble	Amble	Folkestone East and West	Folkestone
Druridge Bay	Widdrington	Hythe	Hythe

Gloucester	Blyth	Grand Redoubt	Hythe
Park	South Shields	Dymchurch	Dymchurch
Whitburn	Sunderland	Greatstone	Greatstone
Seaham	Seaham	Dungeness 6 inch	Dungeness
Seaton Carew	Hartlepool	Dungeness 4.7 inch	Dungeness
Whitby	Whitby	Jury's Gut	Dungeness
Scarborough	Scarborough	Winchelsea	Winchelsea
Filey	Filey	Pett	Rye
Hornsea	Hornsea	Hastings	Hastings
Sunk Island	Humber	Bexhill	Bexhill
Stallingborough	Humber	Cooden	Cooden
Grimsby	Humber	Norman's Bay	Pevensey
Mablethorpe	Mablethorpe	Pevensey	Pevensey
Jacksons Corner	Skegness	Eastbourne	Eastbourne
Boston	Boston	Seaford	Seaford
King's Lynn	King's Lynn	Brighton	Brighton
Hunstanton	Hunstanton	Worthing	Worthing
Brancaster Bay	Brancaster Bay	Angmering	Angmering
High Cape	Wells next the Sea	Bognor	Bognor Regis
Cley Eye	Cley next the Sea	Stone Point	Southampton Water
Sheringham	Sheringham	Southbourne	Christchurch
Cromer	Cromer	Mudeford	Christchurch
Mundesley	Mundesley	Swanage	Swanage
Happisburgh	Happisburgh	Upton	Weymouth
Winterton	Winterton	Abbotsbury	Abbotsbury
Hopton	Yarmouth	West Bay	Bridport
Pakefield	Lowestoft	Lyme Regis	Lyme Regis
Kessingland	Kessingland	Seaton	Seaton
Easton Wood	Covehithe	Sidmouth	Sidmouth
Southwold	Southwold	Exmouth	Exmouth
Dunwich	Dunwich	Dawlish	Dawlish
Minsmere	Minsmere	Shaldon	Teignmouth
Sizewell	Thorpeness	Corbyns Head	Torquay
Aldeburgh	Aldeburgh	Salcombe	Salcombe
Bawdsey	Bawdsey	Looe	Looe
Felixstowe	Felixstowe	Par	Par
Frinton	Frinton	Helford	Helford River
Clacton	Clacton	Newquay	Newquay
Mersea West	Mersea Island	Padstow	Padstow
Foulness	Foulness	Instow	Barnstaple
Shoeburyness	Shoeburyness	Ilfracombe	Ilfracombe
Coalhouse	Thames	Harbour	Minehead
Shornmead	Thames	Portishead	Portishead
No 1 Bastion	Sheerness	Burry Point	Llanelly
Shellness	Shellness	Belan	Caernarvon
Herne Bay	Herne Bay	Walney	Barrow
Margate	Margate		

Batteries with a day role only

Godwin	Humber	Fletcher	Thames and Medway

Needles	Isle of Wight	Wanstone	Dover (later full-time major battery)
Blacknor	Portland		

Close-defence emergency batteries

Inchkeith	Forth	Citadel	Dover
North Sutor	Cromarty	Lydden Spout	Dover
Kincraig	Forth	Capel	Dover
Castle 9.2 inch	Tyne	Hougham	Dover
Frenchmans	Tyne	Mill Point	Folkestone
Heugh	Hartlepool	Newhaven Fort	Newhaven
Pasley	Tees	Culver Down	Isle of Wight
Rainborough	Humber	Nodes 9.2 inch	Isle of Wight
Brackenbury	Harwich	East Weare	Portland
Landguard	Harwich	Renny	Plymouth
Joss Bay	Broadstairs	Peniee	Plymouth
St Margarets	Nr Dover	Roselands	Falmouth
South Foreland	Dover	Half Moon	Falmouth
Fan Hole	Dover	East Blockhouse	Milford Haven

Very few coastal guns still remain emplaced around the shores of the United Kingdom proper. This example is still emplaced near Thorshavn, one of the main ports in the Danish Faroe Islands. The only gun on the British coastline that I know of personally is on the Island of St Kilda. The gun in the picture is a British 5.5-inch Mark 1 naval gun, and some are still emplaced in the Ascension Islands (Eric Bull).

Appendix C

Recognition of coastal defence structures

As mentioned in the section on military architecture, the ability to recognise various remaining concrete structures for what they once were is a valuable asset. This section deals with only a few structures, because to cover all aspects would entail a full-length book on the subject. But it will give a few of the more common structures to be seen near our coastlines and a few extra details as well. Nearly every location and stretch of coastline has its own peculiar differences but overall the basics remain the same.

Recognition 1. Almost any coastline will have somewhere along its length a structure similar to this one which is a beach defence or local defence gun position. The gun involved was frequently an ex-naval model but was sometimes a field piece. Most of these positions rarely used anything larger than about 4-inch guns and most were smaller. A full 360° traverse was the norm. This particular photo shows a common feature of 20th Century coast defences in that the modern position has been built on to an old structure.

1

Recognition 2. While headlands and cliff-tops were unsuitable locations for large-scale troop landings they were often useful for infiltrating commando-style raids or diversions and thus some form of defence was frequently necessary. Consequently such features were often defended by infantry units housed in small bunkers and with light weapons located in small trenches or weapon pits such as this one. Such positions can often be found in mutually-supporting clusters and only rarely in isolation. This hexagonal weapons pit housed a light automatic mortar but it might just as easily have mounted a machine-gun or light anti-tank weapon.

Recognition 3. A typical light anti-aircraft gun mounting position. Note that the hold-fast is low but a full 360° traverse is possible. If it had been a light field piece a higher pedestal would have been used and the surrounding blast walls would have been higher. As it is the surrounding walls have been kept low to enable the gun to be used in a ground role. The bays around the walls were for storing ammunition and one wall is open to enable the gun to be got in and out of action quickly. In many such locations the gun and crew would have been housed in nearby blast-proof bunkers and the gun would only have been run out when an expected pre-invasion barrage had been lifted. Such positions were rarely built in isolation—two or three were the usual minimum.

Recognition 4. There are several features to be noted in this photograph. The walls themselves are specially built anti-tank defences and the shape is characteristic of that function, even though there are many variations. Note how the wall has been built on to an existing structure on the left, again a recurring feature of coastal defences. The gun position does not point out to sea but along the beach and some may be found facing inland. This is not unusual on beach defences and is a common design feature of the Atlantic Wall defences, the gun usually involved being the 4.7 cm Pak 36(t). This gun was specially built for fortress use and many originated in the

4

Sudetenland defence lines which were taken over by the Germans in 1938 and 1939. The drawing shows the type of steel embrasure used by these guns, and additional steel shutters over the embrasure added extra protection—hence the entrant under the position shown in the photograph.

Recognition 5. The two photographs show typical examples of the two main types of observation post. The concrete structure was used for housing direction-finding

5

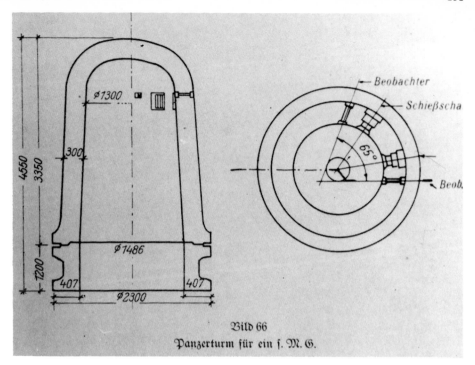

Bild 66
Panzerturm für ein f. M. G.

5

equipment, hence the large slots (the Channel Island towers were a local variation on this theme). The drawing shows cross-sections of a steel cupola used for artillery observations only (ie, visual only), and as they were intended for use at quite short ranges they were frequently heavily armoured. Some even went to the extent of being retractable and on the Atlantic Wall there were many that had been stripped from interior defence lines such as the Maginot Line and the Sudetenland defences. However, both types were used in the United Kingdom and elsewhere. The concrete

6

7

structures usually had their own local defences either built into them or situated in supporting bunkers or trenches.

Recognition 6. While most coastal and beach defences were ideal for daylight use, an attack at night raised problems of seeing the attackers. Consequently most complete defences featured searchlight positions which, in their turn, had to be defended against fire. Special searchlight shelters, often quite large, had to be built and this picture shows a typical example. It is identified as a searchlight shelter by the flat ramps which lead from the landward side of the shelter out to the 'wings'. The searchlights were on wheeled or tracked carriages which were kept inside until needed. When their moment came they were moved out, one to each 'wing' and switched on, still protected on the seaward side by the bulk of the shelter itself. There were several variations on this theme but few went to the length of keeping the searchlights inside a casemate or anything similar. At the very least they were kept in structures built on to the side of towers.

Recognition 7. While beach and local defence guns usually had complete overall protection, coast defence guns were nearly always kept well back from the beaches and thus needed less protection. Consequently most coast defence guns were mounted on open platforms such as this one. The ramp is rather unusual as most defence guns were fixed ex-naval pieces—this one in Jersey mounted mobile 15 cm guns. Again it is unusual to find such installations with only one position—three was the usual minimum for any coastal battery and more often four. Most coastal batteries also had attendant local defence positions, protected magazines and quarters, their own fire control bunkers, observation facilities and signals establishments, so the finding of a gun platform will often indicate that there is, or was, more to be found in the vicinity.

Recognition 8. A typical beach defence bunker on the Atlantic Wall—such structures are unusual around the coasts of the United Kingdom as there was no time to build them when they were needed and no need to build them when there was time. Found all along the Atlantic Wall these formidable miniature fortresses were carefully emplaced along vulnerable beaches, on headlands and at important points. Each usually mounted a 105 mm gun, a 47 mm anti-tank gun (as used on the beach defences in Recognition 4), several machine-guns or machine-gun ports, and

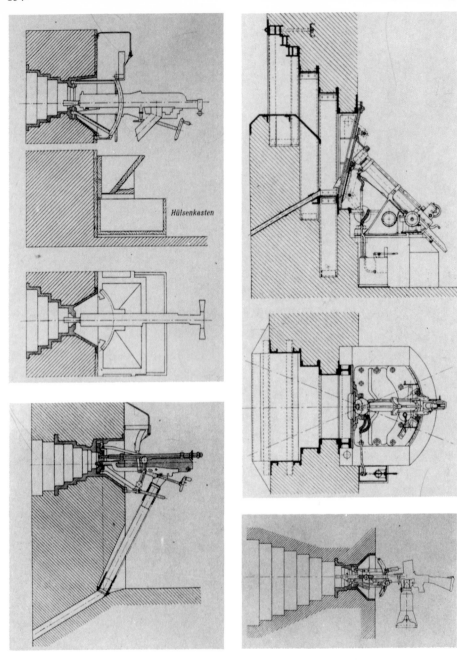

Hülsenkasten

9

a 'Tobruk' stand on the roof. This latter feature was an open sentry position just big enough for one man with a rifle or light machine-gun, and was vacated as soon as a target approached. Sometimes extra defence was given by the addition of an old tank turret on the roof or nearby. Supporting defences were usually scattered around as can be seen from the dilapidated machine-gun position seen in this photograph.

Recognition 9 A, B, C, D. Detailed examination of any modern defence structure will show all manner of defensive measures built in. On beach defences, gun ports face in all directions but every avenue of approach, and especially entry ports and doors, usually have machine-gun ports covering them. The design of these ports is often ingenious and these four pictures show some, and only some, variations. The stepped embrasures are designed to deflect offensive fire away from the gun muzzles whenever possible. Very often extra defensive shutters, operated from inside the gun position, will be found as well. Note how the three machine-guns all have facilities for collecting or disposing spent cartridges and in one instance they are actually ejected down a chute to outside the position. Inside the gun position was often slightly pressurised or had extra piped ventilation to keep away offensive fumes. The mortar was frequently used in defensive positions to deliver vertical fire on to areas which could not be covered by direct fire.

Appendix D

The Dover Defences, 1940-1944

As mentioned earlier in this book one of the many sites which will bear close attention from the historians of our period is the Dover area. I myself have often been intrigued by the importance and involvement of the Dover garrison between 1940 and 1945, but always by reading and findings in libraries and files, and never by actually visiting and looking around the area. But my presence has never been really necessary for, as always in our field, someone was present on the spot to do all the legwork for me. Indeed, most of my queries had already been answered by Eric Bull, who lives in nearby Ramsgate. Eric is a fine example of the type of amateur historian who is motivated by nothing more than a concern at the paucity of information available to the local public on the momentous years of 1940 to 1944 when the Dover area was literally Britain's front line. As his concern grew so did his research and findings. Fieldwork, letter-writing, visiting libraries and various establishments all combined to give him a remarkably comprehensive insight into the organisation, complement and armament of the Dover defences. Interviews and conversations added that final personal touch and his final end-product is a small book which he has personally written and illustrated from his own resources. It is included here, not only as an excellent account of Dover at war, but as another example to be followed by others who might want to carry out similar projects.

It must be said that, despite Eric's work, the Dover region still has many historical secrets to unfold which are worthy of the attention of future researchers. I myself unwittingly uncovered one in the Royal Artillery Institution Library at Woolwich. Hidden among some papers I came across a map showing the distribution of shells which landed in Dover itself from 1940 onwards. A conversation with someone who was in the area at the time revealed that most of those shells were APHE (Armour-Piercing High Explosive) and were thus fuzed to detonate *after* piercing armour plate or something similar. As most of the shells landed on houses or open ground, this was too soft to make the shells explode and thus, to this day, Dover is built over unexploded high explosive projectiles!

The Dover Defences

by E.C. Bull

Ever since the land mass of Britain separated from the continent many thousands of years ago, the geographical position of Dover has made it an obvious landing point for invading forces from Europe. Most of our 'modern' history is generally taken from the point when the Romans invaded and ever since then Dover and its environs have been fortified against invaders to some degree or another. Of all these various fortifications Dover Castle was, and still remains, the biggest and best-known example and over the centuries it has been progressively altered, added to and improved to the extent that it is a mecca for fortification historians. By 1914 the Dover area was well-protected by various batteries of coastal artillery, including the famous Pier Turret with its two massive 16-inch RML (rifled muzzle-loader) guns, and after 1914 more guns were added to protect the harbour which became an important naval base and home of the 'Dover Patrol'. One incidental from this period is the fact that Dover was the recipient of the first bombs to fall on British soil on December 24 1914—two bombs on the 23rd fell into the sea just outside the harbour.

After 1918 the importance of Dover to the Navy declined, and the Dover defences themselves were run down accordingly. Many of the heavy guns of the 1914-1918 period were removed leaving only a few elderly coastal guns of indifferent performance still in place and manned. In 1939 the largest of these were the 9.2-inch guns of Citadel Battery which were limited by their elderly mountings to a range of around 17,000 yards, which meant that they could reach only about half-way across the Channel towards France. Elsewhere were 6-inch and 4-inch guns, and for close-in defence against light and fast naval craft were 12 prs and twin 6 prs. But in 1939 the war was in Europe and there seemed to be no cause for the rapid updating of the Dover defences.

All that changed with Dunkirk. In a little over six weeks the Germans swept across France and were on the coast of the Pas de Calais. From being a quiet backwater, Dover overnight became the front line and drastic measures were taken to reinforce the area. Just after Dunkirk the priority seemed to be defence against imminent invasion and the arsenals and stores of the United Kingdom were scoured for artillery of all kinds to rush to the coast and emplace in hurriedly constructed positions. The array of guns so emplaced was large, and varied from old World War 1 artillery pieces to naval guns taken from ships dismantled after 1918. The Royal Navy generally made a practice of storing any guns that still had a reasonable life left in them when a ship was scrapped, and in 1940 this proved a godsend. Thus naval stores provided numerous 6 pr, 12 pr, 4-inch, 4.7-inch, 5.5-inch and 6-inch guns for coastal defence and, apart from the Dover region, many more were set up around the British coasts. Inland, 49 4-inch guns were fitted on to heavy 6×4 lorries for 'defence in depth' and they patrolled the coastal regions. In all about 510 guns were emplaced or added to the defences of the United Kingdom, some of them 'foreign' such as the French/American 75 mm field guns which were remounted on to coastal defence pivots.

But all these emergency measures were for purely local defence. Defence from afar was not at first catered for as there was none to be had at first. Minds turned to the experiences endured from the attentions of the Paris Guns which fired on Paris from ranges of over 70 kilometres. It was assumed that the Germans had not neglected their researches into such long-range artillery since then and this assumption proved correct. Soon after the Germans occupied the Pas de Calais they moved up long-range railway guns, mostly 28 cm K 5(E)s but also single examples of the 21 cm K 12(E) which had a potential range of 115 kilometres. At the same time survey work began on the sites of coastal batteries which were to house 40.6 cm, 38 cm, 30.5 cm and 28 cm guns, all of them with naval ancestry and sufficient range to fire across the Straits of Dover and deny them to Allied shipping, to say nothing of being able to command a considerable arc of East Kent from Dungeness to Ramsgate.

In June 1940 the Prime Minister, Winston Churchill, called a meeting to consider any possible counter-measures that could be taken against the potential threat of

German long-range artillery. As a result of this meeting the Director of Ordnance met with the Vickers-Armstrong gun design team and it was decided to mount 14-inch Mark 7 guns on extemporised proof mountings originally intended for 18-inch naval guns. These weapons had a range of 47,200 yards (Imperial measurements will be given from here on in order to keep the 'sense' of the original documentation) with a specially super-charged cartridge. The shell so fired weighed 1,400 lb. It was agreed that the Royal Navy would release four barrels which were originally destined for the still incomplete HMS *King George V* Class battleships. Right from the earliest stages representatives of the Southern Railway were involved in the discussions for it was they who would have the unenviable task of transporting the guns and their mountings to their chosen site, which was to be on a golf course above St Margarets Bay.

Work went ahead on the project with amazing speed, with the Prime Minister giving his sanction to all that had been planned. The site was cleared and prepared ready for the ponderous construction of the first 14-inch gun which was delivered on July 13. Despite air raids work continued apace so that on August 3 the first gun was ready for action. It fired its first aggressive round on August 22 1940 and this projectile had the dubious distinction of being the first round fired from Britain to France. It was not long before the 14-inch gun was nicknamed 'Winnie' after the man who had instigated its 'birth'. It was manned by men of the Royal Marine Siege Regiment who were trained at Catterick Camp.

A problem arose with the installation of the second 14-inch gun as it transpired that there was only one 18-inch proof mounting available for use, and indeed it was the only one in the United Kingdom. As that had been used for 'Winnie' something else had to be found for what was to be the gun of 'B' Battery ('Winnie' was 'A' Battery). A quick search soon discovered a likely alternative in the shape of an 18-inch gun mounting which had originally been installed on HMS *Furious* and then removed when she was converted to an aircraft carrier. It had then been fitted to HMS *Erebus* for bombarding the Belgian coast in 1918 but was subsequently removed and used as a trials mounting on the Isle of Grain. The Battle of Britain and the onset of bad winter weather delayed the final completion of the second gun installation until February 1941. It was soon named 'Pooh', and from then on 'Winnie' and 'Pooh' started to fire at the new German batteries in France.

The two guns were installed actually before the German batteries were completed, but it was not expected that they would have to carry the whole offensive burden by themselves. To back them up the Army, under the aegis of Lieutenant-Colonel Cleeve, began a programme of re-activating a number of railway guns that used carriages built during the Great War. The same meeting that instigated 'Winnie' and 'Pooh' also initiated the revival of the railway gun. In 1918 British railway guns were among the best in the world but thereafter they were stored and forgotten— many were scrapped. But in June 1940 it was decided that four of the larger carriages were to be given new guns and moved to the Dover area.

Originally these carriages had mounted 14-inch guns but these had long since been removed. It was proposed that the railway mountings should be modified to take 13.5-inch naval guns which had once more been put aside by the frugally minded Navy. They had been the original main armament of the old *Iron Duke* Class battleships scrapped as a result of the Washington Treaty in the 1920s. In their basic form they fired a shell weighing 1,400 lb but the maximum range was only about 40,000 yards. As this was insufficient to fire usefully across the Channel it was proposed that a new light shell weighing 1,250 lb could be developed quickly which would enable a range of 48,000 yards to be attained. But it was realised that new

A 9.2-inch coast defence gun of the type situated at the Citadel Battery in 1939.

projectiles would take around nine months to develop and produce so, as an emergency measure, the heavier shells would have to be fired using a heavier charge than normal, and the resultant strain on the carriages would have to be endured.

Three railway mountings were altered to take the 13.5-inch barrels. In 1918 these had been given names and they endured after 1940. The three involved were 'Scene-Shifter', 'Peace-Maker' and 'Gladiator'. The fourth mounting was 'Boche-Buster' which had earlier been altered to take the 18-inch Howitzer Mark 1 which had a mere range of 22,300 yards, and was thus retained in the counter-invasion role only. So in early 1941 the defence of the Dover area rested solely on five long-range guns—'Winnie', 'Pooh' and the three railway guns. All five were used to fire at the German positions in France but their efforts were not always successful. For a start, observation of the fall of the projectiles was a very difficult affair and air observation was not often available. All five guns were incapable of quick traverses and were thus unable to be used against such rapidly-moving targets as shipping—the railway guns had virtually no traverse at all and relied on the use of curved rail spurs for laying on target, while the extemporised mountings used by 'Winnie' and 'Pooh' were huge and ponderous affairs, again with little traverse. The role of all five guns was purely defensive, which was just as well for it was not long before a major problem arose with them.

Special super-charge increments had to be added to the normal charges in order for useful cross-Channel ranges to be achieved, and these not only added greater stress to the mountings but also had the more serious effect of wearing out the barrels faster than had been anticipated. For instance, 'Winnie' wore out her first barrel after only 50 rounds had been fired, and these had already been fired before

'Pooh' was even installed. Only four barrels had originally been allotted for the task, after which there would be no more without causing a major disruption to naval construction schedules. Consequently both guns were used less and less, and were eventually reduced to a 'care and maintenance' level, awaiting a task that might arise in the future. Both gun positions were carefully camouflaged and concealment was taken to the extreme of erecting dummy positions some distance away from the real locations. But such concealment was largely wasted as all the erection and subsequent work had been perfectly visible to the Germans on the opposite coast, and it was rumoured that they went to the extent of dropping dummy wooden bombs upon the dummy wooden guns!

Before leaving the railway gun story for the moment, it would be as well to consider the other such weapons in the Dover area. They were all Great War veterans that had been kept on the Army reserve list and consisted of 12-inch Mark 5 howitzers and 9.2-inch Mark 13 guns. Pride of place amongst all these veterans went to 'Boche-Buster' with its huge 18-inch howitzer and, like most of the railway guns, it used the lines of the Elham Valley light railway (which ran roughly north-south along Elham Valley) and was thus well-placed to provide counter-invasion fire to a number of likely beaches and other points. A special spur line was built at Kingston, and the Bourne tunnel was used as a shelter for the equipments in the event of air raids or any anticipated bombardment. The line boasted some delightful place names such as World's Wonder Bridge, Lickpot Bridge and Charlton Park while the Black Robin Pub at Kingston was no doubt a popular stop as well as being the calibration site for the 18-inch howitzer. The line was the preserve of the 2nd Super-Heavy Regiment, RA, while the 4th Super-Heavy Regiment, RA, used the spur lines laid into Golden Wood near Ashford for their 9.2-inch railway guns. But none of the railway guns in the area did anything more than act as morale-boosting propaganda subjects for newsreels and photographs, for the simple reason that none had the range to fire more than even a little way across the Channel. Like the long-range guns at Dover in early 1941, they were purely defensive.

One small sidelight regarding 'Boche-Buster' is worthy of mention and that is with regard to its considerable noise and muzzle-blast when fired. Fortunately its firings were restricted to those essential for training and calibration and the odd shot to impress visiting dignitaries, for whom the Dover Defences tour was virtually *de rigeur*. When a firing was planned the unfortunate inhabitants of the Elham Valley were warned to keep their windows open 'to avoid damage'. But it never made any difference, the windows shattered anyway. Another unfortunate effect of 'Boche-Buster' was on the very fabric of the track and its foundations, for the total weight of the carriage and gun was in the order of 250 tons and, despite considerable re-laying of track and sleepers, etc, moving the beast caused considerable damage.

The defensive steps taken thus far were all rather rushed and improvised measures to meet an urgent need. Weapons such as 'Winnie' and 'Pooh' and the railway guns in no way could be thought of as effective counters to the long-term artillery threat anticipated from France, nor could the Dover defences deny the Straits of Dover to German shipping in the same way as the Pas de Calais batteries threatened to do to Allied vessels. As early as June 1940 planning had begun on emplacing new and modern coastal batteries in the Dover area to replace the rather elderly equipment already there. New installations for 6-, 8-, 9.2-, 15- and even 16-inch batteries were proposed and carried forward. The largest of these was to

Right *Biggest of all the artillery pieces in the Dover area was the 18-inch howitzer mounted on 'Boche-Buster'.*

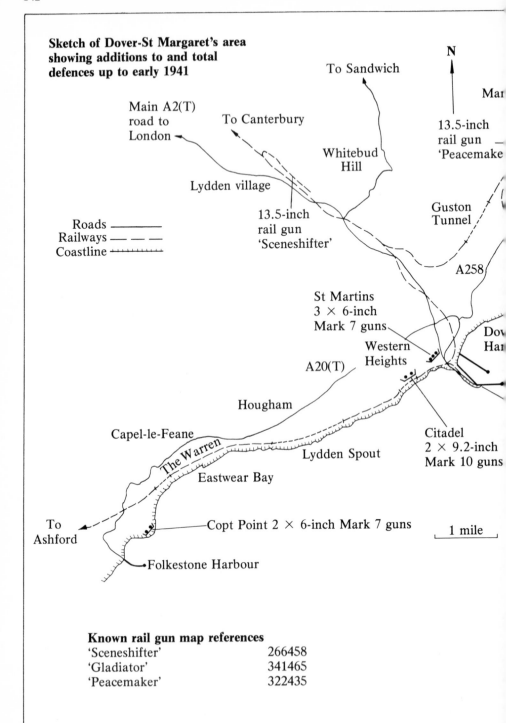

Sketch of Dover-St Margaret's area showing additions to and total defences up to early 1941

N

To Sandwich

Mar

Main A2(T) road to London

To Canterbury

13.5-inch rail gun 'Peacemake

Whitebud Hill

Lydden village

Guston Tunnel

Roads
Railways
Coastline

13.5-inch rail gun 'Sceneshifter'

A258

St Martins 3 × 6-inch Mark 7 guns

Western Heights

Dov Ha

A20(T)

Hougham

Capel-le-Feane

The Warren

Lydden Spout

Citadel 2 × 9.2-inch Mark 10 guns

Eastwear Bay

To Ashford

Copt Point 2 × 6-inch Mark 7 guns

1 mile

Folkestone Harbour

Known rail gun map references

'Sceneshifter'	266458
'Gladiator'	341465
'Peacemaker'	322435

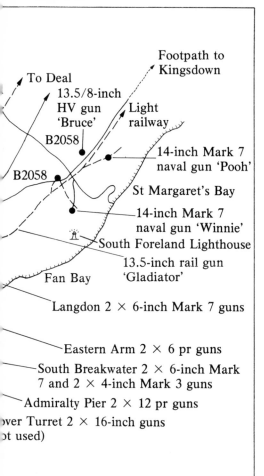

To Deal
13.5/8-inch HV gun 'Bruce'
B2058
B2058
Footpath to Kingsdown
Light railway
14-inch Mark 7 naval gun 'Pooh'
St Margaret's Bay
14-inch Mark 7 naval gun 'Winnie'
South Foreland Lighthouse
13.5-inch rail gun 'Gladiator'
Fan Bay
Langdon 2 × 6-inch Mark 7 guns

Eastern Arm 2 × 6 pr guns
South Breakwater 2 × 6-inch Mark 7 and 2 × 4-inch Mark 3 guns
Admiralty Pier 2 × 12 pr guns
ver Turret 2 × 16-inch guns
ot used)

Battery map references

Copt Point	241368
Citadel	305403
St Martins	315408
Dover Turret	324399
Admiralty Pier	330379
South Breakwater	335405
Eastern Arm	341412
Langdon	339428
'Winnie'	358448
'Pooh'	368454
'Bruce'	361455

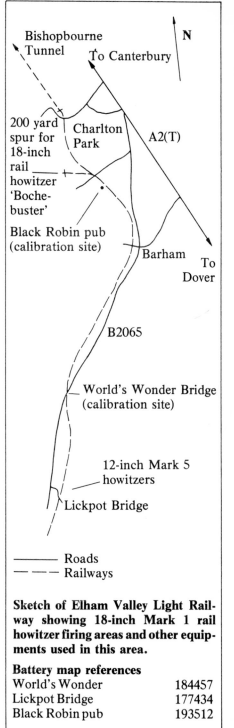

Bishopbourne Tunnel
To Canterbury
N
200 yard spur for 18-inch rail howitzer 'Boche-buster'
Charlton Park
A2(T)
Black Robin pub (calibration site)
Barham
To Dover
B2065
World's Wonder Bridge (calibration site)
12-inch Mark 5 howitzers
Lickpot Bridge

———— Roads
– – – – Railways

Sketch of Elham Valley Light Railway showing 18-inch Mark 1 rail howitzer firing areas and other equipments used in this area.

Battery map references

World's Wonder	184457
Lickpot Bridge	177434
Black Robin pub	193512

have been the so-called 'Hope' Battery of two 16-inch guns of American origin which was planned for the North Foreland. However, it was never built as not only did the proposed site prove unsuitable but the guns never materialised.

The 6-inch guns were to be installed in two three-gun batteries capable of firing to 25,000 yards which was a considerable improvement on the old 6-inch guns already at Dover. Their role was to be anti-convoy work, in which they would be backed up by six 8-inch naval guns with a range of 30,500 yards. This considerable range enabled them to reach almost to the French coast itself, which was to prove invaluable in disrupting German coastal traffic. While the 6-inch and 8-inch guns were primarily destined for use against convoys and light naval craft, larger naval ships would have to be countered by something heavier and for this role four 9.2-inch guns on high angle mountings were to be emplaced. Even so, it was felt that something heavier still was needed to back them up. As a result two 15-inch guns were to be emplaced. Using the expertise gained from emplacing such heavy guns on land mountings at Singapore, the two 15-inch guns were to be the largest weapons ever mounted by the coastal defence artillery batteries in the United Kingdom, and were given a dual-purpose role. Not only were they to engage naval targets in the Channel but they were to have the task of providing a counter to the numerous German batteries in the Pas de Calais.

Work went ahead on all the new batteries but as they were to be modern and fully-equipped installations they were time-consuming to build. The first to be ready were the 6-inch Mark 24 batteries at Fan Bay and Lydden Spout. The former guns were all well protected and concealed in casements while those at Lydden Spout were in open pits. Both batteries had good arcs of fire with the latter having a potentially useful degree traverse in case of a landward attack.

The 8-inch guns selected were the Mark 8** type, which were originally naval guns intended for mounting on 'County' Class cruisers. They were taken over by the Army virtually unchanged and retaining their turret mountings which had a maximum elevation of +70 degrees for anti-aircraft use. Two three-gun batteries were emplaced, one at Capel near Folkestone and the other at Hougham, Dover. Capel was also the site of the main radar station which was later used to such good effect in target-spotting and ranging, but visual observation points for the 6- and 8-inch batteries were built all along the nearby cliffs. (Folkestone also boasted two 6-inch Mark 7 guns placed there as part of the 1940 Emergency Battery scheme— today their site is still in use as a council store and putting green.)

The 9.2-inch battery was to become known as the South Foreland Battery and the guns used there were Mark 15s. The first 9.2-inch guns appeared in 1894 and the Mark 15 was the most modern of a long line. It could fire a 380 lb shell to 31,300 yards but a supercharge was later introduced which boosted the range to over 36,000 yards. This battery was ready in October 1941 and thereafter it bore the brunt of the coastal artillery burden as, from its first shot until September 17 1944, it fired no less than 2,248 rounds. But it was on February 12 1942 that the South Foreland Battery missed its best chance, for on that day the German battlecruisers *Scharnhorst* and *Gneisenau*, accompanied by the cruiser *Prinz Eugen*, made their spectacular dash through the Channel. It was a misty day with visibility down to under five miles when the ships were first picked up by the radar. The gun crews took their posts but no orders to open fire came from the fire control centre. This was for a variety of reasons, not the least of which was that Royal Navy units were attempting some form of offensive moves, with the net result that, when the guns were eventually ordered to open fire, their targets were already steaming away from them at great speed. Nevertheless, three hits were made but the German ships eventually reached safe harbours. It was not one of the coastal artillery's finest moments but the gunners themselves cannot be blamed.

It was a great pity that the 15-inch guns were not ready at the time of the 'Channel Dash'. The two guns involved were still at that time being installed at Wanstone Farm, near St Margarets-at-Cliffe, but neither was ready until the end of May. As mentioned above, the Wanstone Farm battery used a great deal of the expertise gained with 15-inch guns at Singapore and, indeed, the two guns were spares intended for Singapore. To give them their full designations the guns were both Ordnance, BL, 15 in Gun Mark 1 on Mounting, 15 in Mark 3. The barrel of each gun weighed approximately 100 tons and when emplaced the whole equipment, together with its naval-type barbette mounting, weighed approximately 224 tons. To serve the gun there were power rooms, ammunition stores and a host of other structures. Each shell weighed 1,938 lb and the guns had a maximum range of 42,000 yards. Each mounting could be elevated to +45 degrees and traverse was 240 degrees. Such was the scale of operation of these guns that each was served by a single Royal Artillery battery. Number 1 gun was served by 302 Battery, RA, and Number 2 by 320 Battery, RA—both came under the command of 540th Coast Artillery Regiment, RA, and overall control of the Dover area was undertaken by 12 Corps Coastal Artillery under the late Brigadier C.W. Raw. He had his main control

One of the Wanstone Farm 15-inch guns. Particular items to note are the large camouflage nets which show up badly close to, but would be almost invisible from even a few miles away and would thus effectively conceal the gun, and the small tractor used to haul the shell and propellant charges.

'Winnie' in action, actually in September 1944.

room actually beneath Dover Castle, and such was the degree of Navy-Army co-operation on the Dover Defences that the wall separating the two control rooms was knocked down to the benefit of all concerned.

Thus by mid-1942 the Dover defences were ready for anything but, despite the rushed installation of 'Winnie' and 'Pooh', the area was having a difficult war. Ever since the first German rail guns had been moved into the Pas de Calais area in 1940 it had been subjected to a constant drizzle of German long-range artillery shells. As early as August 12 1940 the first shells fell into Dover itself and thereafter the town suffered very badly to the extent that, by 1944, nearly every building on the sea front had been destroyed. Large numbers of the population and all the children had been evacuated soon after Dunkirk but many remained and for them there was no possible warning or defence against artillery fire. The fire of the German railway guns was at first countered by the 13.5-inch railway guns and 'Winnie' and 'Pooh', but their fire was rather 'hit and miss' and few of their projectiles hit anything useful. 'Winnie' did manage one very damaging hit on Calais Harbour but the only immediate result was a heavy air raid on Dover and an extra scattering of shells along the English coast. Perhaps the most remarkable of all the rounds fired against East Kent in 1940 were those fired by the 21 cm K 12(E) which fell near Rainham—Rainham is about 88 kilometres from the Pas de Calais! Fortunately the 21 cm K 12(E) was such an elaborate piece of ballistic machinery that only two were ever built and neither saw very much aggressive use.

By early 1941 the first German coastal batteries were being built in and near the Pas de Calais. All the German batteries used modified naval guns which were housed in armoured turrets, but Hitler himself ordered that turrets were insufficient protection against air attack and insisted that each gun emplacement should be covered by an extra roof of reinforced concrete. The largest of the German batteries was Batterie Lindemann at Sangatte which had three 40.6 cm (16-inch) guns. Next in order of descending size was Batterie Todt, to the west of Cap Gris Nez, which had four 38 cm (15-inch) guns of the same type as those fitted to the *Bismark* and *Tirpitz* (in fact the turrets and guns involved had originally been intended for retro-fitting to the battle cruisers *Scharnhorst* and *Gneisenau* to bring them up to *Bismark* standards). To the west of Boulogne was Batterie Friedrich August which had three 30.5 cm (12-inch) guns, and also in the Cap Gris Nez area was Batterie Grösser Kurfurst with four 28 cm (11-inch) guns. Other batteries had 24 cm guns and scattered around were railway guns from 15 cm upwards and Army artillery units for counter-invasion forces. As each of these batteries was constructed and commissioned they used the distant Kent coastline as a convenient calibration and ranging point and the populations of Dover, Folkestone and Ramsgate suffered accordingly. After the Wanstone Farm Battery guns got into their stride the German guns would often fire retaliation rounds which frequently fell into the Kent town areas causing yet more damage, until it seemed to the suffering townspeople that every time the big British guns fired at some unseen target the Germans deliberately showered large shells on to the easily hit built-up areas. No doubt this did sometimes happen but most of the time the offending shells were 'shorts'. Not all fell short for in November 1942 shells fell around 'Winnie' and 'Pooh' causing some damage to the installations, but even more at a nearby anti-aircraft gun position where 11 men were killed. Both guns were also under quite intensive air attack at times but, apart from a few casualties, they survived.

As soon as the two 15-inch guns were 'commissioned' (and soon nicknamed 'Clem' and 'Jane') the two 14-inch guns were, as mentioned above, gradually reduced to care and maintenance. The same thing happened to the 13.5-inch railway guns which were withdrawn from use by about the middle of 1943 without ever firing any of their long-awaited 'light' shells which would have increased their range. (Some shells were fired as calibration rounds but so few were initially available that they were never fired at France.) By August 1942 the 15-inch guns were firing in conjunction with the South Foreland 9.2-inch battery and it was not long before all six guns were engaging ships in the Channel. Most of these were in small coastal convoys hugging the French coast but the efficient radar in use enabled the fire control centres to engage them with a surprising degree of accuracy. At odd times German blockade runners would attempt to make their own version of the 'Channel Dash' with their precious cargos of special war materials such as chrome, latex and wolfram. One of these was the infamous *Neumark* which got through— others were not so lucky and by the end of 1944 some 26 ships had been sunk by the Dover guns.

Unfortunately, all this activity produced retaliatory fire from the Germans and the towns suffered accordingly. By mid-1944 Dover and the towns nearby were battered almost beyond recognition; not only, it must be said, by the German guns, but also by an almost constant succession of air raids, most of them light after late 1940 but still enough to cause disruption and damage. The forces moved into Dover and the surrounding country in large numbers. Anti-aircraft guns of all calibres proliferated and military establishments sprang up all over the place. Most of the male population was in one form of uniform or another, ranging from the Home Guard to the very active Royal Observer Corps and the Mine-watching Service.

Dover was the home of one of the most unusual artillery pieces ever to be made in the United Kingdom, and to the array of artillery names mentioned above yet another must be added—that of 'Bruce'. The story of 'Bruce' really began with the

Paris guns of 1918 when the Germans managed to increase their projectile ranges by firing them into the stratosphere where the thin air reduced friction against the shell walls and thus enabled hitherto undreamed-of ranges to be attained. The Germans repeated the technique with their 21 cm K 12(E) and in October 1940 the Director of Naval Ordnance, together with Vickers-Armstrong, started the development of a hyper-velocity gun with a muzzle velocity sufficient to fire a shell to altitude and reach out to a range of 60 nautical miles (121,600 yards). Various pilot schemes were investigated before it was decided to go ahead with a 13.5/8-inch solution in which a 13.5-inch barrel would be lined down to eight inches and extended to give a weapon length of 90 calibres, ie, 90×8 inches $= 720$ inches. This length was dictated by the size of the longest gun lathe in the country, which was normally used to process and turn 16-inch guns as fitted in the battleships *Rodney* and *Nelson*. When completed the gun had a 13.5-inch breech and chamber and a long 8-inch barrel, so that a 'normal' 13.5-inch charge was used to propel an 8-inch shell (this calibre being selected as the smallest that could contain a useful offensive payload). It was anticipated that this arrangement would give a muzzle velocity in the order of 45,000 feet per second which would provide the hoped-for range. The gun prototype was built by Vickers-Armstrong and contained in a light armoured housing and equipped with power controls and hydraulic ramming gear. Originally it was intended to site the new weapon on the Isle of Grain for trials but this was changed to a position close to 'Pooh', actually about 500 yards distant. But the new gun, by then nicknamed 'Bruce' (apparently after Admiral Sir Bruce Fraser, a member of the Ordnance Committee), did not point towards France. It was aimed north towards the wide sands near Shoeburyness where the experimental station long established there could closely observe the fall of shot and make accurate measurements. The firing trials were carried out on March 30/31 1943 and the shells fired were 69.6 inches long, weighing 256 lb of which only 26 lb made up the offensive warhead. The maximum range obtained during these trials was 100,000 yards. They were not a great success otherwise as three out of four shells exploded in mid-flight, no doubt due to the great pressures involved. But the worst setback to the project came after only 28 rounds had been fired when it was found that the gun barrel was too worn for further use. This excessive wear was no doubt due to the type of propellant then in use and the trials were not continued. It was not long before 'Bruce' was removed from its rather vulnerable site and returned to an unknown holding point: perhaps the most valuable result from the gun was the considerable mass of research data accrued for possible future use.

But to return to the Dover Defences proper: by early 1944 plans for Operation 'Overlord', the invasion of Europe, were well advanced, and the Dover Defences had a considerable part to play in them. An involved deception plan was drawn up to make the Germans think the main invasion fleet would descend on the Pas de Calais area and it was here the Dover guns were called into use. 'Winnie' and 'Pooh' were brought back to full operational readiness and the 15-inch guns stood ready.

On June 6 1944 all four of the large Dover guns, soon known as the Dover 'Big Four', opened fire on the Pas de Calais batteries. Their fire was not only to prevent the German batteries from firing at the numerous Allied convoys which passed along the Kent side of the Channel, but also to add one extra element of doubt as to the final outcome of the invasion plans. Unfortunately the 'Big Four' were unable completely to eliminate German artillery fire and some Allied ships were hit and sunk. After June 6 things died down a bit but, as the Allied waves crept into France, the fire of the Pas de Calais batteries grew ever more frantic and the East Kent coast once more suffered from their attentions. But the end was not far off. By the end of

July the Royal Marine and Royal Artillery gunners were working together with a degree of efficiency which had until then not been thought possible. In 1940 the two 14-inch guns had been rushed into service without many of the usual calibration and ranging tests usually thought essential but by the end of July 1944 there had been time accurately to range the guns against the wreck of the *Munsterland*, a blockade-runner which had been sunk earlier by the Dover guns. Its hulk provided a useful radar echo that had an added advantage in that it could be used as a 'marker' for fire corrections against the mainland.

Throughout July and August sporadic counter-battery fire was exchanged but on September 17 1944 the final phase of the Dover Defences story began, for on that day all the 'Big Four' began the first coastal battery versus coastal battery duel in the history of artillery. Up till then the British and German guns had swopped shells on many occasions but never in a direct gun-to-gun duel. The final battle was in direct support of a land operation taking place on the other side of the Channel, carried out by the 2nd Canadian Corps against German positions in the Pas de Calais. The task of the Dover 'Big Four' was to prevent the German guns in the area having any effect on the course of events and in that they were entirely successful. In fact they were so successful that one of the Wanstone Farm 15-inch guns was able to score a direct hit on one of the 40.6 cm gun emplacements of Batterie Lindemann—thereafter that gun took no further part in the proceedings. An artillery spotting aircraft was used in this operation. The German batteries continued to fire until they were literally overrun by the Canadian troops but they were unable to have any effect on the infantry operations. By September 20 it was all over.

After that attack there was nothing else for the Dover defences to do. The 15-inch guns alone had fired some 1,243 rounds but they did not stand down until all the British coastal defences were stood down in 1956. The 14-inch guns were soon removed but many of the other Dover defences also survived until 1956, after which they were either handed over for other purposes such as stores and the like, or were abandoned.

Dover itself had a considerable price to pay for its role between 1940 and 1944. Artillery fire alone was the direct cause of the deaths of 103 persons and another 432 were wounded. To this must be added a further 109 killed by air raids with a wounded list of 336. But not only people suffered. Some 80 per cent of all dwellings in Dover were to some degree or another damaged by either shelling and/or bombing—957 houses were completely destroyed. Some houses were hit as many as 13 or 14 times and a few unfortunate structures were hit as many as 27 times. It was a high price for Dover to pay.

What is left now

These notes were made in 1976 and since then some structures have been demolished or have disappeared in other ways but it does provide a useful general guide.

Starting at Folkestone, the two 6-inch emplacements at Copt Point are still in existence and are used as council stores, as are the underground quarters, etc, all guarded by the old Martello tower nearby.

At the 8-inch Capel Battery, just behind the Valiant Sailor public house (an apt setting for ex-naval guns), are the three emplacements with the radar and plotting rooms on the edge of the cliffs overlooking the Warren, a local beauty spot.

Up at Hougham, again one of the 8-inch batteries, are the remains of what was once a large collection of emplacements and other structures. In front of this collection are the three gun-pits of the 6-inch Mark 24 guns of the Lydden Spout battery, with a line of plotting rooms all along the cliffs to Akers Steps. Down the cliffs, hard alongside the railway lines, are two forward spotting rooms.

Coming into Dover, at the extreme edge of the Citadel and by HM Prison 'Borstal', are the three old 9.2-inch Mark 10 emplacements. They are still complete and one can still see where the stanchions that supported the gun platforms were, and also the remains of the platforms. The holding bolts are still in position, complete with the nuts.

At St Martins battery overlooking the harbour can be seen 6-inch casemates. They are very well preserved and look as though they are still ready to receive the guns.

The Pier Turret, although it is rather outside our era, is still very much apparent and there are plans current to restore it to its former state.

Langdon Battery is in a very sorry state but one can still read the sign 'Langdon Battery' as one enters. It is possible to identify nearby 6-inch Mark 7 emplacements and the cartridge and shell positions are still there.

An interesting excursion is to go down the cliffs via Langdon Stairs and visit the fighting searchlight positions tunnelled into the cliffs just above the high-tide mark.

Fan Bay Battery is now no more which is a great pity as until 1974 it was left practically as though the guns had just been removed. But if one cares to clamber down Fan Hole, observation points and sound-ranging gear can still be found. Along the cliffs near this point, just beneath the Fan Bay Battery position, are two entrances down to underground plotting rooms.

Near St Margarets one can see Wanstone Farm where the 15-inch guns were sited. It is possible to see the emplacements clearly from the road but permission must be obtained from the owner for closer observation.

At Townsend Farm the site of the 14-inch naval gun 'Winnie' can still be found. On the Kingsdown side of St Margarets, just off the Kingsdown Road, in a field to the left will be seen all that remains of the 13.5/8-inch gun 'Bruce'. Further along this road and down a small road to the right is the site of 'Pooh'. This site still has its ammunition stores and a closer search will reveal the tracks of the light railway leading back to St Margarets.

One other relic in the area is a section of armour plate from one of the German Pas de Calais batteries. It is situated on the Dover sea front and was handed over to the town by the Canadian Army. Inscribed on the plate is the number of shells fired at Dover from that particular gun emplacement, along with the date of each firing.

A 15-inch gun barrel can be seen outside the Imperial War Museum.

(In order to get the bulk of Eric's work into the confines of this book I have had to omit some of his maps and other findings, not the least of which is the considerable amount of data he has amassed on the guns themselves. I hope Eric will forgive me for this. *TG*.)

Appendix E

The Home Guard

The Home Guard—Dad's Army—had their origins in the Local Defence Volunteers, first formed in the desperate days of May 1940 when a German invasion was deemed imminent. Then any man between 16 and 65 who was 'capable of free movement' was considered eligible to join and join they did, in their thousands. They had no uniforms, apart from locally improvised armbands, and they had few weapons except their own shotguns or sporting rifles, and most carried simple clubs or loaded sticks—the much-quoted pikes came a lot later. Gradually they were issued with uniforms, and weapons were obtained from the USA, mainly old .30-inch rifles and machine-guns from World War 1 surplus stocks.

In time they came to appear more and more as military units rather than the organised mobs of the early days, and British industry gradually started to equip them with simple weapons which had some form of anti-tank capability. These weapons included the Northover Projector, the Smith Gun and the Blacker Bombard, and by 1941 they were capable of giving a good account of themselves against any invader. Knowing their localities intimately they were excellent potential guerilla warfare exponents, but as the danger of invasion receded their role gradually turned to the manning of rocket batteries for anti-aircraft defence and in some areas they took over beach and coastal batteries. Throughout the war they manned pillboxes, kept guard over important road junctions and possible invasion routes, and they constantly trained for a task they gradually began to realise they would never have to carry out. But they kept at it and their spirits remained high until they were disbanded in 1945.

Every locality had its own Home Guard platoon or larger unit and these local associations can form the basis for excellent preparatory research projects. In a very few places the local or county museum still retains the records of 'their' Home Guard, but more often than not they have been destroyed or lost. This can be at least partially corrected by your own investigations—there is no shortage of raw material around—and all it needs for you to complete a very worth-while project is a bit of effort.

This picture was taken at a small-arms range in the west of England and shows Home Guard soldiers on a machine-gun course. Visible is just about every machine-gun type in use by the HG.

Above *Taken on Merseyside during the last year of the war, these Home Guards are manning a 3-inch rocket projector, a task given to the Home Guard in order to free regular manpower for other roles.* **Below** *This shot was taken on the factory roof of the Fairey Works at Heaton Mersey and shows an extemporised light AA gun formed from an ex-aircraft 20 mm Hispano cannon.*

Above *Another Hispano cannon used as a light AA gun. The extemporised sights indicate that it would probably have been of little use in its intended role unless tracer ammunition was used, and that was always in short supply during 1940 and 1941. Doubtless the gun provided some form of morale protection.* **Below** *Anti-tank grenade training in progress outside the Fairey Works.*

Above *A lunchtime demonstration of a Northover Projector to an avid audience made up of Fairey workers.* **Below** *A Home Guard unit, which one, unfortunately, is not known, proudly parades with their Smith Gun. The Smith Gun was one of the simple weapons produced during 1940 to provide some sort of defence quickly and cheaply. It had a smooth-bore barrel and a limited range but would have been more than adequate for street and close-quarter fighting. An unusual design feature was that in action it was tipped over on to one of its large wheels, the one nearest the camera, and it then had a full 360 degree traverse and the bonus of overhead protection from the wheel itself.*

Right *In the early days local ingenuity often produced some odd defensive devices. This picture shows the CO of the Dorking Home Guard holding a simple mortar that was designed and made locally for the sum of £1 8s 4d. It closely resembles the improvised mortars used by the modern Provisional IRA in Northern Ireland.*

Below *Another example of Home Guard ingenuity was provided by the Southwick Home Guard in Sussex who built this trailer to give their 0.30 Browning machine-gun more mobility. The same trailer was used to carry their Northover Projector.*

A few useful addresses

Architecture

Channel Islands Occupation Society:
Jersey Branch: M. Ginns, 'Rangistacey', Rue des Sablons, Grouville, Jersey.
Guernsey Branch: K. Tough, 'Gladclift', Ruette Braye, St Martins, Guernsey.
The Fortress Study Group, D.R. Barnes, BSc (Econ), 24 Walters Road, Hoo, Rochester, Kent, ME3 9JR.

Pillboxes

Henry Wills, 5 Washern Close, Wilton, Salisbury, Wilts, SP2 0LX.

Vehicles

Warnham War Museum, Warnham, Nr Horsham, West Sussex.
Historic Commercial Vehicle Club, M.J. Banfield, Iden Grange, Cranbrook Road, Staplehurst, Kent.
This club, as its title shows, deals mainly with commercial vehicle conservation but has a thriving military section.

Military Vehicle Conservation Group, Peter Grey, 15 Tarring Road, West Worthing, West Sussex.
39-45 Military Vehicle Group, Clive Moles, 13 Valley Rise, Desborough, Northants.
Four-Wheel Drive Club, J. Gearing, 220 Park Lane, Frampton Cotterel, Bristol, Avon.

Cartridges

Collector Cartridges, Kingston, Canterbury, Kent.

No doubt many readers will want to add their views and knowledge to the contents of this book. I will be very happy to hear from them. Any corrections, comments and leads to new projects, sites, restorations and odd vehicles, etc, will be most gratefully received at the address below:

T.J. Gander,
5 Carpenters,
Billingshurst,
West Sussex RH14 9RA.